The Sea People
of Sulu

The Sea People
of Sulu

A Study of Social Change
in the Philippines

H. ARLO NIMMO

CHANDLER PUBLISHING COMPANY
An Intext Publisher
SAN FRANCISCO • SCRANTON • LONDON • TORONTO

Library of Congress Cataloging in Publication Data

Nimmo, H   Arlo.
   The sea people of Sulu.

   (Studies in social and economic change)
   Bibliography: p.
   1.   Samals (Philippine people)   2.   Sulu Archipelago
——Social conditions.   I.   Title.
DS666.S3N54   301.29'599'9   70-179034
ISBN 0-8102-0453-3

To
My Parents,
Howard and Jane Nimmo

CONTENTS

TABLES

MAPS

FOREWORD

It is the intention of this series to present monographs each of which deals with a particular group of people, without seeking to define that phrase too narrowly. Monographs focus on, for example, an African ethnic group, a South Asian caste village or group of villages, and the people of a Pacific island. Each monograph is self-sufficient in its own right and not directly dependent on others in the series, and each is written by an anthropologist who has recently carried out field research in the area concerned.

The focus of each study is on economic, political, and cultural changes, their causes, processes, and consequences during the twentieth century among the selected group of people, and with particular reference to the preceding two decades or so. The primary aim is to describe the changes that have occurred and to give an explanation of the processes involved and their implications. Although broader generalizations (including comparative references to cases and processes elsewhere) are not neglected, it is not a major concern of the series to seek to establish or promote a particular theoretical approach or conclusion. Each author is asked to go beyond description and to make an analysis involving theoretical considerations according to his own preferences.

In the preparation of this series we recognized the necessary diversities of research interests and opportunities, and of theoretical orientation, but nevertheless asked each author, as far as possible, to include the following:

a. in relatively brief outline, the description of a fairly clear and relevant socioeconomic baseline from which to present the account of change (for example, immediately prior to the establishment of colonial rule, or of the achievement of independence, or of the introduction of some major, radical innovation of a technological or social nature);

b. an account of the factors responsible for producing and developing changes and of the agencies through which those factors operated; the initial reactions of the people to these factors and agencies, including the perceptions of the people about them;

c. a description and analysis of the various changes, taking account both of time sequences and of different aspects or parts of the society and culture; the identification of key roles such as those of innovator, entrepreneur, and reactionary (we asked for description to be reinforced, if possible, with quantitative data on such matters as crop production, school attendance, religious converts, and voting in elections);

d. a consideration of sequences of changes within a single field of activity (such as agriculture) and the extent to which there were concomitant changes in other fields of activity (for example, the association of agricultural change with modes of economic cooperation, family organization, religious beliefs and practices, and political action);

e. a summing up of the processes of change in the context of anthropological theory.

We encourage each author to make a serious attempt to cover a wide range of social and cultural changes among the selected people, but acknowledge his legitimate preference to emphasize certain processes of change on which he has most data and theoretical interest.

P. H. GULLIVER
D. J. PARKIN

ACKNOWLEDGEMENTS

If the names of all persons who in some way assisted in the preparation of this book were mentioned, the list would probably exceed the length of the book. Consequently, only a few of the most indispensable will be mentioned here.

I could never have survived the physical and emotional ordeals of fieldwork without Father Emile Laquerre and Father Henri LaVallee, the Oblates of Mary Immaculate priests of Bongao. Twice they nursed me to health through critical illness, and innumerable times they offered their home and companionship when they were most needed during the loneliness that is so often anthropological fieldwork. I can never hope to adequately repay their kindness, and consider myself fortunate to have known men of their great stature.

The cooperation of the Bajau was, of course, key to whatever success my research may have. Among the boat-dwellers, Masarani generously shared his floating home with me as he taught me the ways of his people. Antonnio Alari, friend and invaluable informant, served the same role among the house-dwelling Bajau. If nothing else, these two men proved to me that deep friendships can transcend cultural barriers. The hundreds of other Bajau who assisted me must remain unnamed; I trust they remember my gratitude.

Many other people in the Philippines should be mentioned: members of the Philippine Air Force, who befriended me, fed me, and bunked me many times at their lonely Sanga-Sanga outpost; the Oblate priests throughout southern Sulu who kindly took me into their conventos when I arrived, often hungry and sea-soaked; the Medical Mission Sisters in Bongao who provided me with medicines and taught me new meanings of the word charity; Tarabasa Idji, friend, assistant, and sometimes interpreter. In Hawaii, Dr. Alice G. Dewey spent much time with my data and offered me important insights in her very human way; Dr. Katharine Luomala was most helpful in the laborious business of writing-up. And in Los Angeles, Marian Post and Jo Ann Johnston spent many hours in typing the finished manuscript. The successes of the research are theirs: I alone am accountable for the shortcomings.

And finally, I gratefully acknowledge the foundations that supported my research: the East West Center (1963–1964); the National Science Foundation (1965–1966); the Wenner-Gren Foundation for Anthropological Research (1966–1967); the Carnegie Foundation (1967); and the National Defense Graduate Fellowship Program (1967–1968).

The Sea People
of Sulu

1. Introduction

One of the most unusual peoples of the ethnically diverse Philippine nation is a small group of boat-dwellers who inhabit the shallow seas of the Sulu Archipelago. The Bajau, popularly known as "sea gypsies" or "sea nomads," are one of several enclaves of boat-dwellers found scattered throughout insular Southeast Asia. Accounts by early Chinese and European travelers reveal that boat-dwellers once inhabited the waters of the Mergui Islands, Singapore, Jahore, Bangka, and Celebes, as well as the Sulu Islands. Today most of these people have abandoned their boat-dwelling way of life to become amalgamated into land-dwelling populations. Pockets of boat-dwellers still remain in the Mergui Islands, Celebes, and Sulu; but these people, too, are rapidly leaving their sea-borne homes, and, if present trends continue, the sea nomad culture will eventually disappear from Southeast Asia.

This book specifically deals with the changes which have occurred among one group of sea nomads, the Bajau of southern Sulu, as they have abandoned their boat-dwelling lives to become house-dwellers. The data were collected during twenty-four months of field research among the Bajau of the southern Sulu Islands in the Republic of the Philippines. A year was spent among each of two groups of Bajau, namely, the boat-dwellers of the Tawi-Tawi Islands and the house-dwellers of the Sibutu Islands. This study is primarily descriptive of the structural changes wrought upon Bajau society by the abandonment of the nomadic boat-life and the acceptance of a sedentary house-life.

It has been stated frequently that the world produces no new ideas, but rather rearranges past thoughts into new configurations. I do not intend to discuss the philosophical validity of the statement, but simply wish to acknowledge that many of the ideas which led to the interpretation of social change presented in this book came from other men. I have found particularly enlightening the views of some social structuralists; thus, a review of their ideas is a necessary beginning to this book.

Raymond Firth (1951) was one of the first to take a stand on structural change and to suggest a reexamination of the models which social anthropologists construct to describe social structure. With minor alterations, Firth accepts the classic definition of social structure as a model constructed from the jural rules of society, which he feels provide the "continuity principle of society." He introduces, however, the concept of "social organization," which is the "systematic ordering of social relations by acts of choice and decision." Social structure sets a "precedent and provide[s] a limitation to the range of alternatives possible— the arc within which seemingly free choice is exercisable is often very small. But it is the possibility of alternative that makes for variability. A person chooses, consciously or unconsciously, which course he will follow. And his decision will affect the future structural alignment. In the aspect of social structure is to be found the continuity principle of society; in the aspect of organization is to be found the variation or change principle—by allowing evaluation of situations and entry of individual choice" (p. 40). Thus change is possible in any social structure because of the alternative behavior always available to members of the society. Presumably, when enough members of a society begin to choose an alternative pattern of behavior, the structure of that society will alter accordingly. Conse- quently, to deal with structural change, the social anthropologist must deal with social structure—the jural rules of society—as well as social organization—the variety of actual behavior displayed by members of society.[1]

This view of a social system as consisting of both a social structure, or jural rules, and a social organization, or the manipulation of those jural rules, is particularly useful in explaining the changes which have occurred among the Bajau. Although the structure of the sedentary, house-dwelling Bajau society at Sitangkai appears upon first examination to be a radical departure from the nomadic, boat-dwelling life these same people lived twenty years ago (as exem- plified by the Tawi-Tawi Bajau today), it is my contention that the geneses of practically all the seemingly unique characteristics of the house-dwelling society are to be found in the behavioral patterns of the nomadic, boat-dwelling society. This position offers an explanation for the easy, undisruptive changes which have occurred among the Sitangkai Bajau with the abandonment of the nomadic boat-life.

An example may best illustrate its relevance to the Bajau case. Among the boat-dwelling Bajau, marriage between first cousins is permissible so long as the cousins are not patrilateral, parallel cousins or have not been close playmates or reared in the same household. However, among the sedentary Bajau at Sitangkai, all first-cousin marriage is beginning to meet with general disapproval. At first blush, the prohibition of first-cousin marriage at Sitangkai seems a radical depar- ture from the marriage practices of the boat-dwelling Bajau. However, upon closer examination, it appears that the initial acceptance of sedentary house-living (which has fostered the development of large matrilocal, extended families occu- pying single dwellings) has led to the prohibition of first-cousin marriage, since many first cousins live in the same household or live in neighboring households and are therefore not proper marriage-partners by traditional Bajau mores. Thus, the change in jural rules regarding marriage at Sitangkai has its roots in the traditional alternative patterns in the boat-dwelling society.

Equally relevant to the Bajau case are the contentions of students of cognatic societies (such as Goodenough, Appell, Scheffler, and Keesing) that the different roles an individual holds throughout the society, which cross social categories, allow for and give direction to change. For example, upon marriage a boat-dwelling Bajau continues to belong to his personal kindred (a large, amorphous category of cognates), but also belongs to his wife's personal kindred. He may decide to remain in his father's moorage to live among a group of cognates, a localized segment of his personal kindred; he may decide to live among a comparable group of his mother's kinsmen; or he may decide to live among any of several such groups of his wife's kinsmen. The point is that he has membership in several groups (none of which is mutually exclusive), and the group (or groups) which he decides to affiliate with is determined by his personal ambitions or wishes. And since individual wishes and ambitions tend to change over time, the structure of Bajau society tends to alter accordingly. Thus, as many recent critics of social-structure studies have pointed out, an adequate description of a society must present not only the dominant patterns of behavior but the deviation from those dominant patterns—that is, the alternative patterns of behavior found in the reality of social life. Only then is the concept of social structure able to deal with the changing, dynamic nature of social life.

Granted that change is possible within a structure because of the alternative behavioral choices available to members of the society, the position as stated here offers little in the way of explanation of why individuals begin to choose differently from the way they have chosen in the past. The stimulus for pursuing different patterns of behavior among the Bajau appears to have come from their recently more intimate associations with the land-dwelling people of Sitangkai, as well as from the innovations of individual Bajau, often sparked by desire for economic advancement.

To the casual observer, the house-dwelling Bajau at Sitangkai would probably represent a classic example of acculturation, a group of people who have borrowed cultural elements from an invading, dominant society. It is, however, misleading to attribute the changes among the Sitangkai Bajau to acculturation alone, at least as that word is traditionally defined. In the first place, the Bajau have lived in varying degrees of intimacy with the land-dwellers for unknown centuries during which time the two societies were doubtless influenced by one another. Thus, even though only in recent years have the Bajau and land-dwellers lived together in a single village, their relationships today are only a more intimate continuation of past relationships. Like almost all societies of the world, the Bajau have always been in contact with other peoples, and the so-called acculturation process has always been operative among them; consequently, it alone cannot explain the recent changes in their society. As Robert F. Murphy (1964) has so ably argued, acculturation is an ordinary feature of almost every social system. And because it is so broadly defined, acculturation contributes little as a theoretical concept to a better understanding of the processes of social change; to say that acculturation has occurred tells little more than that social change has occurred. More recently, Fredrik Barth (1967) has taken a similar stand on acculturation studies. Like Murphy, he maintains that acculturation studies tell little about the processes of change and, indeed, sometimes obscure the actual processes by describing new behavior as elements "borrowed" from another culture. Barth illustrates his position with data from the Fur of the southern Sudan. He notes that some of the Fur people who live near Arabs have a family structure more like that of the Arabs than of the more traditional, isolated Fur. Upon first glance, this seems an obvious case of acculturation, or borrowing. However, closer examination reveals that the "new" pattern of Fur family structure was always possible in their traditional society, but the economic patterns of the traditional society seldom made it practical.

Nonetheless, neither Murphy or Barth, nor other critics of acculturation studies, would deny that change does occur when two cultures previously not in contact with one another come together, or when two cultures with a long history of sporadic contact become more intimate with one another. Their disagreement is based on how such change comes about. Traditional acculturation studies are noticeably reticent regarding the processes by which acculturation occurs, but rather reveal the end result of the meeting of two societies, with the impression that "elements" of culture have been "borrowed" and somehow reworked to fit the patterns of the borrowing culture (Beals 1953). Critics of acculturation studies want to know more about the vague processes of borrowing.

It has long been recognized that when two societies come in contact and if one is superordinate to the other (as the land-dwelling Muslims are to the Bajau), the superordinate society may provide models for change to the subordinate society. And, although the subordinate society may eventually display features that are similar to those of the dominant society, it contributes little to the understanding of social change to state simply that these features have been borrowed from the other culture. In fact, it may be misleading, or even false, to do so. For example, as mentioned, one result of the Bajau contact with the land-dwelling Muslims has been the emerging prohibition against all first-cousin marriage, rather than a prohibition which formerly included only marriage of patrilateral parallel cousins.[2] However, if the Bajau were confronted with a patrilineal society which also forbade patrilateral-parallel-cousin marriage, the traditional Bajau prohibition against such marriages would most likely be intensified. In either case, the real or the hypothetical, students of acculturation may claim that the changing marriage practices of the Bajau were borrowed from the society they encountered. However, varying prohibitions against all types of first-cousin marriages in certain circumstances are found in traditional Bajau society; thus, rather than borrowing the prohibitions, the Bajau would simply have reemphasized certain traditional patterns to make them more congruent to the superordinate model.

This position does not deny, however, that elements of culture are sometimes borrowed by one society from another. This has, in fact, happened among the Bajau in the realm of religious behavior. The Sitangkai Bajau have consciously learned Islamic ritual from their land-dwelling neighbors, a case of obvious borrowing, the syncretic result of which has many parallels in Afro-American religious behavior, where African ritual and deities have been blended with Christian ritual and deities to form a uniquely New World religion. But it is misleading to say that even these elements are borrowed; such a simplistic explanation underplays the often complex reworking and reinterpretation of traditional patterns which must occur.

Innovation is another common, catch-all word which frequently appears in the literature on social change to explain the origin of new behavior. I do not deny the validity of the process in bringing about change, but rather wish to reexamine the manner in which it normally comes about. It is well known that relatively few "new" discoveries are made in the world, if discoveries are defined as additions to knowledge. However, the reinterpretation and rearrangement of past discoveries into new inventions is commonplace, as is witnessed every day in the modern world. Thus, the child who builds a hitherto unknown structure with his erector set has not discovered anything new, but he has invented a new structure —he has manipulated known elements into a new arrangement. The innovators to whom culture change is often attributed also manipulate known parts into configurations, much like the child with his erector set. Obviously, some individuals do come up with new discoveries that may revolutionize the social system, but the majority of innovators rely upon existing knowledge for their inventions. Such has certainly been the case among the few Bajau who have been responsible for the innovations which have brought about radical changes in their society. An example is needed. Twenty years ago, a bright and energetic Bajau headman in Sitangkai apparently realized that the principal barrier to his ambitions in Sulu society was that he and his people were considered pagans by the surrounding Muslim people. To remedy the situation, he sent his youngest son to learn Islamic ritual and then built a mosque in which the son, the first Bajau imam, could begin to proselytize. The new mosque quickly gained a large following of Bajau, and the consequent acceptance of Islam significantly changed Bajau society. The headman's innovation represents no new discovery. Rather, he merely utilized elements of his own culture and the nearby Muslim culture to establish a new institution in Bajau society. It is my contention that most innovation is of this sort, and especially in the Bajau case. The cultural inventory of an individual (which includes elements of the cultures around him with which he is familiar, as well as those of his own culture which he knows) provides the material for innovations. Thus, innovation, like most social change, is germane to the cultural tradition of its producer.

My position throughout this discussion has been that, unlike Athena who emerged full-grown from the head of Zeus, new social behavior can be traced through a finite number of steps to its origin—usually in the traditional society. Confrontation, or more intimate association, with a second society may provide models for behavior or may open opportunities which make formerly less popular alternatives now more popular and may create new possible configurations, thereby setting about processes of change; but the genesis of most seemingly new behavior can be found in the traditional society. These seemingly new patterns of behavior emerge from the alternative patterns of the traditional society, which were always available when the dominant patterns could not be followed. Consequently, to deal with social change, the anthropologist must not only know the jural rules of the society, but must also know the allowable deviations from those rules. Rather than viewing acculturation as the borrowing of certain cultural elements, it can be better understood as the provision of models of new behavior which set in motion new arrangements of traditional patterns in an attempt to approximate the new model. And similarly, innovators use the traditional cultural inventory to create new manifestations of the traditional design. Obviously, this is not the entire story of change. Sometimes societies are forced to accept new patterns of behavior for which there is no parallel in their tradition; sometimes unprecedented discoveries are made which revolutionize social systems; and sometimes elements of culture are consciously borrowed which bring about subsequent changes in the borrowing society. But in cases of cultural change which are not forced and which are not the result of contact with an alien, intruding society, I contend that change most often follows the lines I have outlined.

NOTES

1. Llewellyn and Hoebel (1941) have found a similar distinction useful in their discussion of law. They speak of societal norms upon which most law is based, but also recognize tolerable leeways— deviations from the norm—which are also accepted as legitimate behavior.

2. Although patrilateral-parallel-cousin marriage is a preferred marriage form among most Muslims throughout the Arab world of the Middle East, it meets with disapproval among many Islamic and non-Islamic peoples of Southeast Asia and apparently represents a pre-Islamic tradition in that part of the world.

Part One

THE BOAT-DWELLING BAJAU
OF TAWI-TAWI

2. Habitat

The Sulu Islands, where field research for this book was conducted, lie north of the equator between latitudes 4° 30' and 6° 50' and between east longitudes 119° 10' and 122° 25'. Major islands within the archipelago include Jolo, capital of Sulu Province, Siasi, Tawi-Tawi, and Sibutu. Volcanic and coral islands with extensive reefs characterize this southermost province of the Republic of the Phillippines. The equatorial maritime climate of Sulu has a yearly average temperature of 79.6° f. The islands experience monsoon seasons—the northeast monsoon in the winter months and the southwest monsoon during the summer months—but the monsoon seasons are not as pronounced as they are in continental Southeast Asia.

The islands are inhabited by two major ethnic groups, the Taosug and the Samal, as well as the Chinese and Christian Filipino minorities found in most of the port towns. The Taosug occupy the most fertile islands of the Jolo and Siasi groups and portions of some of the southern islands, while the Samal dominate the islands of Tawi-Tawi and Sibutu, as well as numerous smaller islands throughout the island chain. Both groups are nominal Muslims, with the degree of acculturation to orthodox Islam varying among members of each group.[1] The Taosug have always been the politically dominant group in Sulu and still maintain that position today. The Samal-speaking population is much more diverse than the Taosug. Members range from sophisticated Muslim hadjis, who have made the pilgrimage to Mecca, to the pagan, boat-dwelling Bajau, who still spend nomadic lives in tiny houseboats. The name *Bajau* is not commonly used in Sulu to identify this boat-dwelling Samal people, but is often used in Borneo and Celebes to identify the boat-dwellers of that area, as well as other Samal-speakers. I have chosen to use the name because it is already established in the literature, it does not have the offensive connotations to the Bajau that some of the other local names do have, and it distinguishes the boat-dwelling Samal from the other Samal people of Sulu. *Bajau*, then, shall be used throughout this book to identify the boat-dwelling Samal population of Sulu, those who still occasionally use the boat as living quarters, and those who have only recently abandoned their boat-dwelling. These Bajau people have been reported as far north as Surigao, Davao, and Zamboanga on Mindanao Island, in almost all the major island groups of Sulu, in eastern Borneo, and on numerous Celebes coasts.

The Tawi-Tawi island group of Sulu takes its name from the long, narrow

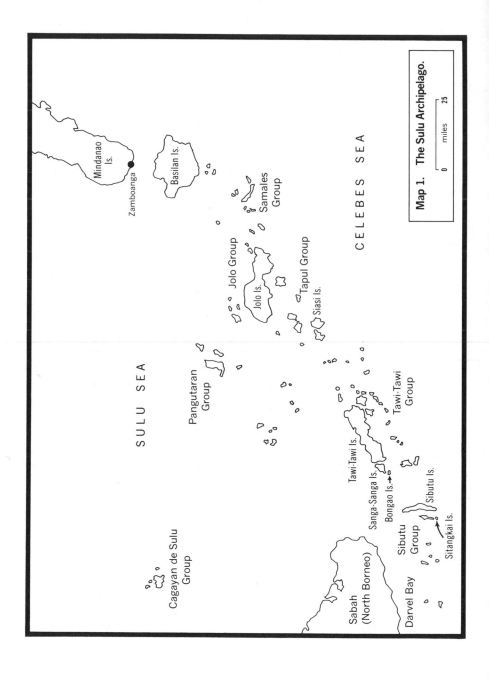

Map 1. The Sulu Archipelago.

0 miles 25

island which stretches in a northesast-southwest direction for twenty-five miles. The verdant forests and rugged volcanic peaks of the island provide a mountainous backdrop for the dozens of small, coral islands flanked about its southern shores. For unknown centuries, its human inhabitants have chosen to live in pile dwellings built along its miles of coast, and, even today, except for a few notable penetrations, the interior of the island is still virgin forest. To the north and west of the island are the deep waters of the open sea, dotted with rich fishing grounds well-know to Tawi-Tawi's seafaring population. Compared to other seas of the earth, these waters are calm and gentle, but nonetheless, during the seasons of the monsoons only the most hardy venture upon them. To the east and, especially to the south of the island, the seas are shallow and filled with myriad coral islands and reefs which make navigation by large ships virtually impossible. At high tide, the waters are as varicolored as only coral seas can be, but at low tide the great, sprawling reefs lie ugly and exposed. It is among these southern reefs and islands that the Tawi-Tawi Bajau have carved their unique ecological niche; their small houseboats ply the waters as regularly and as persistently as the fishes themselves.

The 1960 census of the Philippines does not provide a population breakdown by language or ethnic group for Tawi-Tawi, but probably more than 75 percent of the population is Samal, 20 percent is Taosug, and the remaining 5 percent, Chinese and northern Christian Filipino. The large number of Samal-speakers is somewhat misleading in that it connotes a cultural uniformity which is not entirely the case. Although a general "Samal culture" may be attributed to Tawi-Tawi, nonetheless, almost each island of Samal-speakers is somewhat different from all others. Dialectical differences, occupational specializations, value systems, material culture, religious beliefs, and, in some cases, physical differences, tend to set off the various groups. As a result, the Samal-speakers normally identify themselves by their islands, sometimes even by villages, rather than by *Samal,* which, because of its generic nature, has little value as identification among them.

By far the most unusual group of Samal-speakers is the boat-dwellers, the so-called Bajau. In fact, their uniqueness led earlier observers to describe them as a people separate from the remaining Samal population, but this is not the case, and they are best regarded as a subculture of the general Samal culture. Their most obvious distinctions from the land-dwelling Samal are their boat-dwelling, their "pagan" religion, and certain physical features which can be directly traced to their boat-dwelling. All of these traits mark them as a lowly, outcast group, in the eyes of the Muslim land-dwellers. In Tawi-Tawi, the Bajau number approximately 1,600 and represent only about 4 percent of the Tawi-Tawi population. Their moorages are all located in the western half of the Tawi-Tawi Islands, and, except for occasional fishing trips, they rarely leave these waters. The Tawi-Tawi Bajau are among the most conservative of all the Sulu Samal and probably reflect much of preIslamic Samal culture. Their sea-borne homes, which effectively isolate them from the land-dwelling peoples, seem most responsible for this conservatism; it is significant in this respect that other Bajau groups in Sulu who

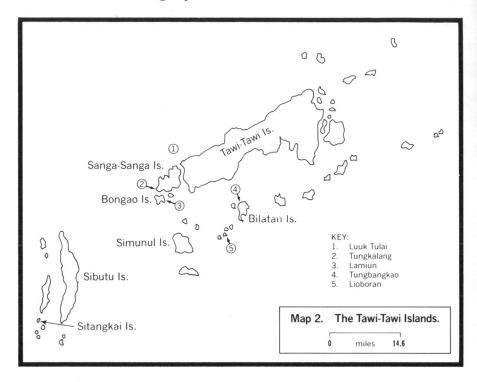

Sanga-Sanga Is.

Bongao Is.

Bilatan Is.

Simunul Is.

Sibutu Is.

Sitangkai Is.

KEY:
1. Luuk Tulai
2. Tungkalang
3. Lamiun
4. Tungbangkao
5. Lioboran

Map 2.   The Tawi-Tawi Islands.

0   miles   14.6

have abandoned the boat-dwelling life to become house-dwellers, have become, or are quickly becoming, amalgamated into such Islamic Samal cultures as the Sitangkai Bajau. Although greatly influenced by Sulu Islam, the Tawi-Tawi boat-dwellers are still regarded as pagans by the surrounding Muslim peoples.

Lone Bajau houseboats and occasional clusters of houseboats can be seen at any time throughout the Tawi-Tawi waters. However, such small groupings generally consist of Bajau on fishing trips or en route to some other destination and cannot be considered permanent Bajau settlements. Five sites are recognized as permanent moorages by the Bajau; these are permanent in that some houseboats are always found there, though in varying numbers. These five moorages surround the seas most commonly exploited by the sea folk (see Map 2).

The northernmost of these moorages is located on the southwestern tip of Tawi-Tawi Island near the land village of Luuk Tulai. It is known among Bajau by the name of the land village and consists of an average of twenty houseboats and about a half-dozen poorly-constructed temporary houses. About eight miles from Luuk Tulai is Tungkalang. Considerably larger than Luuk Tulai, this moorage usually has about forty houseboats and twenty-five pile dwellings built by Bajau who are in the process of abandoning the boat-dwelling life. Lamiun is a small Bajau moorage at the edge of the port town of Bongao. A dozen or so houseboats are usually found here, as are about eight pile dwellings built by more sedentary Bajau families. A fourth moorage, Tungbangkao, is about seventeen miles east of Lamiun near the northwest point of Bilatan Island. About thirty

A Bajau man returns to Lioboran, the smallest moorage, with a boatload of cans filled with potable water from Tawi-Tawi. In the midday heat, the others at the moorage are probably napping inside their houseboats.

houseboats are usually found at this moorage to supplement the forty houses, about half of which belong to non-Bajau (land-dwelling Samal) who have recently moved to the village from various places in eastern Tawi-Tawi. The fifth Bajau moorage is about six miles south of Tungbangkao. Known locally as Lioboran, this moorage has no houses and normally has about twenty-five houseboats.

Although each of the Bajau moorages is in some respects unique, the five share several common features. Each flotilla is located on a protected reef, partly exposed at low tide, which serves also as a source of edible marine life. This reef may be very small, as at Lamiun, or it may extend for several miles, like the one at Tungbangkao. Part of this exposed reef, or a nearby beach, is used for boat-building and other work by the adults and as a play area by the children. Generally, several shallow channels are found among the boats, in addition to one deeper channel which serves as a main passage for boats entering and leaving the moorage at low tide. Throughout the moorage area, poles stuck into the reef are used for mooring the boats. The sea-folk are usually found only a few hundred yards from land villages, and relations between the two groups are normally symbiotic in nature, with the boat people trading fish for the vegetables and fruits of the land-dwellers. With the exception of the land-dwelling Samal population at Tungbangkao, no non-Bajau people live in the moorages. Only Tungbangkao has a few small stores operated by the land-Samal fish buyers; the other moorages have no retail stores of any sort.

Visitors to Tawi-Tawi would probably note other Bajau moorages. For example, a flotilla of eight or ten houseboats may moor for a week or so at a particular anchorage as they fish the nearby waters; however, after exhausting the waters, they return to their home moorage or move on to other fishing grounds. In no sense can these flotillas be considered permanent moorages. During the northeast monsoons some Bajau boats moor near certain land villages, where they plant small plots of dry rice on land owned by land-dwelling friends, but after the harvest they return to their home moorages. As a result of these temporary moorages, it is difficult to make any hard-and-fast statements regarding Bajau settlements.

The five main moorages appear to have been Bajau settlements for a good number of years, but, should any sort of trouble arise, they could disappear overnight. About ten years ago, a Bajau flotilla regularly moored near the land-village of Karundung on the southeastern part of Sanga-Sanga Island. A group of Taosug outlaws from Jolo attacked the land village, killing seventeen persons. Within a matter of hours after the news was learned, the Bajau boats dispersed —some to Bongao to form the present village of Lamiun, and others to the Bilatan villages. During my first visit to Tawi-Tawi in 1963, a sizable Bajau flotilla was located near northern Sanga-Sanga, across the channel from Luuk Tulai. After I left, four Bajau men died mysteriously enough to convince the boat-dwellers that evil spirits were plaguing the moorage and that it was no longer a safe place to dwell. When I returned to the site in 1965, not a single Bajau boat was moored there.

Apparently throughout their history in Tawi-Tawi, the small numbers of Bajau have never given any government serious pause. The Bajau were never fully incorporated into the Sulu sultanate. The Spaniards had little influence in Sulu, and even less among the Bajau. American administrators found the Bajau population small enough to ignore while they attended to the more pressing problems of the land-dwellers, and, similarly, the government of the independent Philippine nation has had enough problems in Sulu without concerning itself with the affairs of a handful of boat-dwellers. Thus, their small population and their nomadic boat-dwelling habit have been important factors in the retention of their traditional way of life.

The population of a single Bajau moorage varies greatly at different times of the month and at different seasons of the year. For example, on a Monday of an October week in 1965, a wedding had attracted 120 houseboats to the moorage of Tungkalang; by Thursday of that week, only 28 houseboats remained. During the season of the northeast monsoons, the winds sometimes build up swells in the open sea which break over the protective reefs of Luuk Tulai and Tungkalang to cause considerable agitation in the reef waters and occasional damage to houseboats. As a result, during this season many Bajau choose to leave these moorages to fish the calm Bilatan waters or to moor near other land-dwelling villages more protected from the destructive breakers, where they sometimes plant dry rice on borrowed land.

Fishing cycles also determine Bajau movements. During the spring tides of the full moon, seas spill over the normally exposed reefs of Bilatan to attract fish from the deeper waters of the newly available feeding grounds. Awaiting their arrival are Bajau from all over Tawi-Tawi, including many from the western moorages who monthly make the trip to Bilatan at full moon. As the moon wanes and the differences between high and low tides are less dramatic, other types of fishing become more practical. At the time of the neap tides, the Bilatan reefs are again the scene of intensive fishing, in the form of communal fish drives practiced by the Bajau when fish are attracted to the reefs in great schools for feeding. Tides, winds, and, of course, fish must be properly disposed during the daylight hours to make this type of fishing feasible; therefore, during the neaps of many months when drives are practiced, many Sanga-Sanga Bajau travel to Bilatan to join in. When the moon disappears completely, the Bajau engage in net fishing with pressure lanterns. This type of fishing is lucrative on many reefs throughout Tawi-Tawi and contributes to much Bajau movement; Bilatan Bajau regularly seek the fish on Sanga-Sanga reefs, whereas the Sanga-Sanga people equally regularly visit the Bilatan reefs for the same purpose. Many other types of fishing are practiced during the month, but the above types attract the greatest number of fishermen at any single time.

The deep seas to the west of the Sanga-Sanga moorages have several fishing grounds which yield large fish to the hook-and-line fisherman, some of whom engage almost exclusively in this type of fishing and rarely travel to the Bilatan reefs. At one time, the reefs of the Basun Islands (northeast of Luuk Tulai) apparently attracted almost as many Bajau as the Bilatan reefs presently do; however, in recent years the area has been rumored to be the hangout of Jolo outlaws, so Bajau fishermen have avoided those reefs. More Sanga-Sanga Bajau travel to the Bilatan reefs for fishing than do Bilatan Bajau to Sanga-Sanga; nonetheless, in spite of the rich fishing grounds in their home waters, many Bilatan Bajau regularly visit the deep-sea fishing grounds of the Sanga-Sanga moorages. In addition, shark fishing attracts many of them to the seas off Sanga-Sanga during the northeast monsoons.

Those few Bilatan Bajau who wish to practice agriculture during the growing season of the northeast monsoon must temporarily reside near Sanga-Sanga or Tawi-Tawi moorages, since the dry, rocky islands of Bilatan do not allow this type of cultivation. Even the Sanga-Sanga Bajau frequently moor near a land village where a land-dwelling friend permits them to use his land for their small gardens.

Ceremonies contribute to much Bajau movement. Kinsmen are expected to attend each other's ceremonies of marriage, healing, and incision, and, since any Bajau's kinsmen are scattered among the five major moorages, a single ceremony in one of the moorages attracts visitors from the others. Not surprisingly, the ceremonial cycles complement the general movements of the fishing cycles: the Bilatan moorages hold their ceremonies during full moon, apparently to take advantage of the presence of many visiting fishermen already in the area, whereas in the Sanga-Sanga moorages ceremonies are held during the period of no moon, when the inhabitants have returned from the full-moon fishing at Bilatan and when many of the Bilatan people are in the area to sell their full-moon catches in Bongao.

The two small cemetery islands near Bilatan Island, Bunabunaan and Bilatan Poon, also account for some Bajau movements. Since all Bajau are buried on these islands, a death at any of the moorages means that an entourage of mourners must travel to one of the cemetery islands for the burial. In addition, the Bajau religious beliefs demand that periodic visits be made to the graves of deceased relatives.

Because the Bilatan Islands produce no cassava, the Bajau vegetable staple, and have no potable water, it is necessary for these Bajau to make periodic journeys to Tawi-Tawi or Sanga-Sanga to obtain these necessities. Furthermore, the Bilatan Islands have no trees suitable for boat-building. Consequently, if a Bilatan Bajau needs to construct a new boat or repair an old one, he usually moves to one of the Sanga-Sanga Bajau moorages which are located near forests with trees suitable for boat-building. Rather than attempt to pull the large logs back to his home moorage, he normally remains at the Sanga-Sanga moorage until the boat is completed.

The nomadic territory of the Tawi-Tawi Bajau is difficult to delimit, since some Bajau have traveled almost the entire length of the Sulu Archipelago, while others have never been outside the Tawi-Tawi area. However, most Bajau travels are limited to the vicinity of Tawi-Tawi, with occasional fishing trips to Sitangkai, and the nomadic territory most commonly exploited by a Bajau generally does not exceed twenty-five miles in any direction from his home moorage.

Bajau men travel more extensively than Bajau women. Almost all the Tawi-Tawi Bajau men have been to Sitangkai (a distance of 40 miles), whereas fewer have traveled to Siasi (75 miles) or Jolo (100 miles). Several Bajau from Tawi-Tawi have traveled to Zamboanga (200 miles), and a considerable number have visited Bajau villages in the Darvel Bay region of Sabah (75 miles).

Much journalistic ink has been spilled on the reportedly senseless wanderings of these "sea gypsies" who are usually depicted as aimless wanderers drifting a carefree life over romantic seas. Such is certainly not the case. A touch of wanderlust may account for some Bajau travels, but most are undertaken for practical reasons of necessity and are patterened, as well as predictable.

NOTES

1. The Islam found in Sulu is a variant of the Sufi sect and was apparently introduced at the end of the fourteenth century by missionaries from Malaya and Sumatra. In recent years, missionaries from the Middle East have introduced elements of modernist Islam in Jolo, but their influence has been little felt in Sulu beyond that city.

3. The Household

The independent, nuclear family of a man, his wife, and their children is the basic unit of Bajau society. It consequently is not surprising to find that the strongest, most enduring, and most important kin relationships are those fostered within this unit, called *mataan* by the Bajau. The nuclear family is the only face-to-face grouping of individuals that endures over an extensive period of time, and even its span is limited by the lives of its members and the marriages of its offspring. Although regularly associated with a larger grouping of kinsmen, the nuclear family is extremely self-sufficient. Much of its time is spent traveling or fishing alone away from the larger Bajau community, and, even when at rest in a moorage, the isolation provided each houseboat by the water separating it from others acts effectively to allow a great deal of privacy to its occupants.

A survey of Bajau households reveals two basic features: (1) The household ideally consists of a single nuclear family, and any variation of this is either temporary or an adjustment to a fragmented nuclear family; and (2) each broken nuclear family adds persons, so that it approximates the structure of the nuclear household. Reasons for this are practical and realistic. First, the size of a Bajau houseboat limits the size of the household, since the average living area of a houseboat is only about ten feet long, five feet wide, and four feet high; consequently, few houseboats are large enough to accommodate more than a single nuclear family, even by the Bajau cramped definition of comfort. Secondly, the Bajau household has a fairly well defined division of labor between husband and wife; essentially, the husband provides sustenance and protection, while the wife cares for the household and the children. While it is not impossible for a widow or widower to live alone, it is difficult and often taxes their immediate kinsmen, who must frequently fill the vacant role. As a result, widows or widowers remarry as soon as possible or form alliances with kinsmen who are left in similar circumstances.

Although the most common composition of households among the boat-dwelling Bajau is that of the nuclear family—that is, husband, wife, and their unmarried offspring—with an average of five members, Table 1 reveals that considerable variation is found within this common structure.

TABLE 1. HOUSEHOLD COMPOSITION OF BOAT-DWELLING BAJAU .

	number of households
nuclear family	103 (78%)
nuclear family and additional unmarried members	
nuclear family and husband's widowed father	1
nuclear family and wife's widowed mother	6
nuclear family and wife's widowed mother and divorced sister	1
nuclear family and wife's widowed mother and widowed sister	1
nuclear family and husband's adult nephew	1
nuclear family and husband's male patrilateral cousin	1
TOTAL	11 (8.3%)
extended family	
nuclear family and married son and family	4
nuclear family and two married sons and families	1
nuclear family and married daughter and husband	2
nuclear family and mother and father of both husband and wife	2
widow and children and her nephew and wife	1
TOTAL	10 (7.6%)
fragmented family	
widower and children	1
widow and children	2
widow, her two sons, her two teen-aged brothers, and her widowed father	1
widow	1
widower and his grandson	1
widow and her children and her widowed mother	1
two widows (second cousins) and children of one	1
TOTAL	8 (6.1%)
TOTAL	132

A biological rather than structural variation of the nuclear family is the case when a man and his wife adopt children. Not uncommonly, a childless couple raises an orphaned child or takes a child or two of a sibling who has more children than he can manage. Sometimes they may be the only children in the household, and sometimes they may have adoptive siblings, but in either case they are treated as biological offspring. Probably there were more cases of adoptions among the Bajau than I was able to discover, since such children are normally referred to by the term used also for biological offspring, and their adoptive status is not significant in the family structure or sentiment. Consequently, unless pressed to do so, a Bajau rarely mentions that a child is adopted.

Frequently an aged adult, a widow or widower, will attach himself to a nuclear household. Most commonly, this is one parent or both parents of either the husband or wife. Occasionally, even an aged couple may join a nuclear family household, but usually, as long as they are both alive and still able, an old couple lives alone until the death of one. If an aged person has several children, he normally moves among their several houseboats rather than staying with one child permanently. There are some cases, however, where an aged adult has chosen to remain permanently with one of his married children, either because there is no space for him elsewhere or because of close emotional ties with that particular child. In rare cases, an aged person lives alone.

Several closely related adults who have been left without spouses and who constitute "fragmented families" (Table 1) sometimes form a household for their mutual economic and social benefit.

Orphaned, unmarried siblings of either the husband or wife are sometimes attached to nuclear family units. Normally, these are the youngest members of their families and are staying with siblings only until they marry and form their own households.

Much diversity is revealed in where each household, whether an independent, nuclear family or a reconstituted or variant form of it, prefers to moor its houseboat. By far the most dominant Bajau residence pattern may be called, for lack of a better term, ambilocal, a general term which covers a number of variations. For the few truly nomadic Bajau it refers to their lifelong movements among the several Bajau moorages and fishing grounds in Tawi-Tawi. For couples who otherwise reside at a single moorage, it refers to those movements which monthly take them away from the moorage in pursuit of fish. For some couples it is a conscious decision to spend part of the year in the home waters of the husband and the other part in the home waters of the wife. For still other couples, it refers to their seasonal residence near certain fertile islands where they practice agriculture.

Because of the frequent movements of Bajau houseboats, the residence pattern in a Bajau moorage on any single day is different—and sometimes dramatically different—from the pattern found on any other day.

TABLE 2. RESIDENTIAL PATTERNS AT TUNGKALANG.

type of residence	Nov. 1965 number of couples		Dec. 1965 number of couples		Jan. 1966 number of couples	
uxorilocal moorage[1]	14	(23%)	10	(29.4%)	8	(19.5%)
virilocal moorage	10	(16.4%)	8	(23.5%)	10	(24.4%)
natolocal moorage	14	(23%)	8	(23.5%)	10	(24.4%)
neolocal moorage	17	(27.9%)	5	(14.7%)	8	(19.5%)
virilocal moorage/virilocal household[2]	3	(4.9%)	1	(2.9%)		
uxorilocal moorage/uxorilocal household	1	(1.6%)	2	(5.9%)	1	(2.4%)
uxorilocal moorage/virilocal household	1	(1.6%)			2	(4.9%)
natolocal moorage/virilocal household	1	(1.6%)			2	(4.9%)
TOTAL	61		34		41	

1. Uxorilocal moorage: the married couple lives in its own houseboat in the moorage of the wife's parents.
2. Virilocal household: the married couple lives in the houseboat of the husband's parents.

Table 2, constructed from surveys of residence taken at the moorage of Tungkalang on three different occasions, illustrates the changing nature of Bajau residence.

If one were to survey Bajau public opinion as to the preferred pattern of postmarital residence among Bajau, he would discover, as I did, that most Bajau profess the ideal that after marriage the couple should spend the first few months moving between the moorages or houseboats of both sets of parents, and then eventually settle down to married life in the moorage of the wife—that is, an initial ambilocality which develops into a more permanent uxorilocality. However, like many social ideals, their stated preference does not always reflect reality, and more practical considerations actually determine the residence of the Bajau.

An initial ambilocality is typical of most marriages. Since newlyweds are often from different moorages, the ambilocal practice allows them to become acquainted with their new in-laws and at the same time relieves a single household of the strain of having to support and find space for an additional person. Sometimes the couple may forego the initial ambilocality and live in the houseboat of a kinsman who needs a male or female to complete the household unit. In one case, this was the groom's mother's widowed sister, who needed an adult male in the household and had space for the extra couple. In another case, it was a widowed man who needed his new daughter-in-law to assume the female responsibilities of his household. Sometimes, if one set of parents has a small and crowded houseboat, the couple may spend all its first months with the other set of parents, which has more space for them. But, whatever the case, the couple expects, and is expected, to have its own houseboat within a year or so after marriage, and most usually do.

Residence becomes even more complicated after the couple acquires its own boat. Some Bajau seldom leave a single moorage, whereas others spend almost their entire lives traveling among the five Bajau moorages in Tawi-Tawi; most Bajau fall somewhere between these two extremes. Those Bajau who rarely travel beyond their home moorages are normally those who have married persons from those same moorages. Often these people are less dependent upon fishing as a livelihood than most Bajau and practice boat-building or agriculture. What fishing they do is limited to the nearby waters, and, except for rare fishing trips to other parts of Tawi-Tawi or visits to the cemetery islands, they seldom leave the moorage. They consequently represent the stable core of the moorage population.

Other considerations may influence a couple's decision to spend most of its time at a single moorage. If one of the couple has few and insignificant kinsmen, the couple normally moors at the moorage where the most important kin ties are. Similarly, if for some reason the couple is on unfriendly terms with the kinsmen of one spouse, it usually moors at the moorage of those kinsmen with whom both are friendly.

A virilocality found in some couples is related to ecological factors. Bajau men living in the western moorages—Luuk Tulai and Tungkalang—most commonly practice deep-sea fishing in the nearby fishing grounds and less comonly do gill-net fishing on the few and small reefs of the area. The reverse situation is found in the eastern moorages—Tungbangkao and Lioboran. Here the extensive reefs allow for profitable net fishing, and rarely do the men practice deep-sea fishing. As a result, those men who grow up in one of these two areas are most familiar with the fishing techniques which most profitably exploit that environment. And, since successful fishing is obviously important in Bajau society, most men prefer to fish those waters where they can use familiar techniques. As a result, when men more familiar with one fishing method marry outside their home waters, most commonly the wife goes to live in the husband's home moorage, where he can most profitably fish the waters. Women's work is less specialized and allows greater freedom of movement.

The couples with neolocal residence frequently have moved to the new moorage after being frightened or driven away from another moorage by land-dwellers. Some listed in the neolocal category also represent couples who are staying in a moorage for only a few days en route to some other destination.

The Bajau contend that for a good marriage it is best to marry relatives, and most do. Indeed, if one were able to completely unravel the web of kinship among the Bajau, he would probably find that all Bajau couples are related in some manner. Bajau are free to marry all relatives except siblings of parents and grandparents, grandparents, and, of course, members of the nuclear family. First-cousin marriage is permissible, except between patrilateral parallel cousins, whose marriage would be considered incestuous unless they had performed a special ritual which involved throwing certain possessions of minor value into the sea. Also, any first cousins who have been reared together intimately are considered improper marriage-partners.

TABLE 3. MARRIAGE PATTERNS AMONG BOAT- DWELLING BAJAU.

genealogical relationship	number of couples
patrilateral parallel first cousins	8(5%)
matrilateral parallel first cousins	9(6%)
cross-cousins	14(9%)
second cousins	30(19%)
second *kamanakan*[1]	14(9%)
related, but exact relationship unknown	47(30%)
uncertain of whether relationship exists	7(5%)
unrelated	26(17%)
TOTAL	155

1. Second *kamanakan:* a relationship of persons separated by one generation in the second degree of collaterality, such as the relationship between ego and the child of his first cousin.

Table 3 reveals the variation found in Bajau marriage patterns among 155 boat-dwelling couples.

Although romantic love is no prerequisite to marriage in Bajau society, many young couples are in love at the time of their weddings. These are the couples who have expressed their desire for marriage to one another through their parents, who have taken care of the formalities of the arrangement, or those not uncommon couples who have eloped rather than waited for the formalities and possible opposition to their marriages. Since Bajau youth are rarely forced into distasteful matches, attraction between the couple characterizes most marriages. After the novelty of the marriage wears away, the romantic love is frequently replaced by a genuine, deep, mutual affection. If it is not, the marriage may end in divorce, or, if a child is on the way, the two learn to tolerate one another.

Deep sentiment between husband and wife seems to be fostered by the intimacy they share by being together virtually all their adult lives in a small houseboat. Very rarely is the Bajau husband away from the houseboat overnight, and commonly he is with his wife and children twenty-four hours of the day. And, since the houseboat is often at sea, separated from the larger Bajau community, it is not surprising that extremely intimate and close ties characterize the nuclear family.

The husband is the recognized head of the household, but most matters are discussed with the wife before any decisions are made. Most commonly the wife is in charge of the small finances each family maintains, which she parcels out for purchases and payments. The husband is in charge of fishing, repairing and maintaining the boat, and making and repairing fish nets and other equipment; the wife is also in charge of cooking, preparing cassava, and gathering firewood from the beaches and edibles from the reef and frequently assists in fishing. Both are actively involved in caring for the children, although infants are, of course, cared for almost exclusively by the wife.

If the husband or wife should die, the surviving spouse expresses real as well as conventional grief at the death. Because Bajau have so little property, the distribution of the dead spouse's property follows only loosely defined custom. When her husband dies, a wife inherits all his property, but she normally redistributes some of it among family members. Male children usually claim his fishing equipment, while the houseboat continues as the wife's home. Sometimes the houseboat is destroyed at a man's death, but only in cases of extreme grief or if the boat is not greatly needed by the living. Similarly, a woman's property normally passes to her husband. What jewelry she may have goes to her daughters, or to her sisters if there are no daughters. An aged couple usually has few belongings left by the time one or both have died, having long ago either given them away to children or worn them out. Personal items of any deceased, young or old, such as clothing, betel boxes, and sometimes jewelry, are placed in the grave with the corpse.

If the married couple finds the marriage distasteful and decides that even the children born to them are not reason enough to maintain an unhappy home, divorce is the frequent way out. Incompatible personalities, barrenness, irresponsibility, and interfering relatives are the most common causes of divorce. If divorce occurs shortly after marriage, the brideprice or a portion of it is returned to the groom's family. Money and goods acquired by the couple, and sometimes even the children, are divided between them. Table 4 summarizes Bajau divorce patterns.

TABLE 4. DIVORCE PATTERNS AMONG BOAT-DWELLING BAJAU.

number of divorces	number of married men	number of married women
0	126 (76%)	122 (79.2%)
1	34 (21%)	25 (16.2%)
2	5 (3%)	6 (3.9%)
3	0	1 (0.6%)
TOTAL	165	154

The intimacy that breeds close ties between husband and wife is responsible for the same sort of ties and sentiments between parents and children. Children are greatly desired in Bajau society for emotional, as well as practical, reasons. Indeed barrenness is a just cause for divorce, and those barren couples who do not want divorce frequently adopt children from more fortunate siblings. The few children a Bajau family does have are cherished even more because of the high rate of infant mortality. There appears to be no preference for male or for female children, and most couples agree that an equal number of each is ideal, since then both husband and wife will have assistance in their work.

Sibling relationships are characteristically intimate and protective. When the family houseboat is at moorage in one of the Bajau moorages, Bajau siblings spend the daylight hours playing together with other moorage children on the nearby beach. But, when the family is away from the moorage, the only playmates usually available for the child are his siblings, and as a result of this periodic separation from the Bajau community brothers and sisters become very dependent upon one another. Older girls frequently assume most maternal responsibilities for younger siblings while the mother is occupied with a newly born infant. If a child somehow acquires food or some item of childhood value, he invariably shares it with his brothers and sisters, but feels no compunction to share it with nonsiblings who may be watching hungrily as he gorges himself. In serious childhood quarrels between two nonsiblings, the siblings of each often become involved, since brothers and sisters usually assist one another in such instances. This intimacy between siblings frequently continues even after marriage, for they prefer to moor their boats together and work as a sibling group.

As noted, the Bajau household sometimes includes additional members, such as aged adults, unmarried siblings of either the husband or wife, or married siblings of either the husband or wife. So long as the aged are physically active and mentally alert, they are vital and respected members of the household. But when they become senile or physically inactive, or both, they are largely disregarded by the other members of the household. They are, however, never maltreated, because of the responsibility children feel toward their parents and because of the belief that old people can curse others with bad luck and illness. Often old Bajau people retain their prestige within the family and moorage because of their knowledge of ceremonial ritual and curing lore. Some old women enjoy renown as midwives. For the most part, the Bajau aged do whatever small jobs they can and then sit back to be cared for by their children.

Unmarried adult siblings of either the husband or wife are expected to assist in the household duties appropriate to their sexes. They assist in disciplining and caring for the children in a parental role, but their position in the household is usually regarded as temporary, and they expect, and are expected, to leave when they marry.

Additional couples in a household are also regarded as temporary members. They, too, assist in duties appropriate to their sexes and discipline and care for one another's children. The crowded houseboat resulting from extended-family households discourages their formation, and they usually last only as long as it takes one of the families to acquire its own boat.

4. The Family Alliance Unit

Although the Bajau nuclear family is extremely independent, it is not an isolated unit unto itself but, rather, periodically attaches itself to a larger social grouping—especially during those periods when it is at one of the moorages. When a Bajau family arrives at one of the five moorages, it normally anchors near the houseboats of whatever kinsmen are there. Usually these kinsmen are siblings of either the wife or husband and are the main reason the family has chosen to stop at the moorage. This group of married siblings who normally moor together in a Bajau moorage and assist one another in work and ceremonies is the second most important social unit in Bajau society, second only to the nuclear family. Although the Bajau call such a group *pagmundah,* a word meaning a group of boats traveling or mooring together, I shall refer to it by the more descriptive term *family alliance.*

The family alliances follow no single structural type, except that they are usually no deeper than two generations and are rarely extended collaterally beyond siblings. The unit may consist of a married man and his several married sons, a married man and his several married daughters, or a married man and his several married sons and daughters. Or it may represent the adults of a single generation—several married brothers, several married sisters, or several married brothers and sisters. However, not all married siblings who reside in a single moorage are necessarily members of the same alliance. For any number of reasons, such as family quarrels, social prestige, or economic factors, married siblings may choose to align themselves with the siblings of their spouses and never act together in a single alliance.

Of the 25 alliance units I surveyed, 1 is composed of two nuclear families, 6 are composed of three nuclear families each, 10 are composed of four nuclear families each, 7 are composed of five nuclear families each, and 1 is composed of six nuclear families. Six consist of married siblings, one consists of married brothers, and five consist of married brothers and sisters. Seventeen are two generations deep; 11 of these consist of a married man and his married children, an extension of the nuclear family; 6 are married siblings and their married child or children. Two are three generations deep; in both cases, they are a married man, his married children, and his married grandchild or grandchildren. Thus, the most common Bajau family-alliance unit is two generations in depth and consists of four nuclear families. The average nuclear family has five members, which provides an approximate twenty persons to each Bajau alliance unit.

Within the family-alliance units, work teams are formed for certain activities. Sometimes these work teams—for example, fishing groups—consist of all the adult males of the family-alliance unit, whereas at other times only two or three members may form such a group. In general, the family-alliance unit provides a group of closely related, trusted persons from which work teams are formed.

Factors important in determining the composition of the work teams, as well as the family-alliance units, include compatibility, occupational preferences, and age. Obviously, only persons who can get along well can work well together. Also, if members of an alliance unit have different occupational interests they will rarely be together in a work team. And since certain fishing techniques require the efforts of several able-bodied men, a family-alliance unit must have several men of this age among its members. If siblings satisfy these requirements, the Bajau work team consists of such siblings or their affinal counterparts. Otherwise, one seeks less closely related persons for alliances. However, I encountered no cases of alliances between nonkinsmen, either in work teams or family-alliance units —partly, no doubt, because, if forced to do so, a Bajau can trace a kin connection to almost every other Bajau in Tawi-Tawi. The Bajau ideal is to align with siblings, and most family-alliance units and work teams realize this ideal.

Because of the frequent movements of the individual nuclear families, the composition of a family-alliance unit is constantly changing. While in his home moorage, a man normally forms an alliance with those of his own siblings who may be there, but, when in his wife's moorage, he is a member of a unit composed primarily of her siblings. While mooring at moorages different from those of his own or his wife's, he ideally forms alliances with siblings of his own or his wife's who moor there or with less closely related persons. When it is remembered that almost each nuclear household of any single unit is extremely mobile, some appreciation of the fluidity of the units may be gleaned.

Single Bajau households begin to break from traditional alliances as their members marry and form their own households. Once a man has married children, he tends gradually to dissolve alliances with his siblings in favor of forming alliances with his children. Eventually this alliance completely replaces his earlier ones, and he never again participates in a unit with his former partners. Most commonly, he acts as leader of the newly formed unit, but as he becomes older he relinquishes this position to a younger member. With his death, the tie with the earlier alliance unit is completely dissolved.

The less nomadic households of the moorages add an element of stability to the otherwise fluid family-alliance units, because it is around these more sedentary households that the nomadic households cluster. These sedentary households, as noted earlier, are those families who rarely travel beyond the waters of the home moorage. Often both spouses are from that moorage and, if they fish, they are content to fish the nearby waters. Frequently, however, they are not fishermen but boat-builders or agriculturalists, who have no need to follow the fishing cycles. Because they are almost always at the home moorage, their less stable siblings, when they arrive at the moorage, form alliances with them. However, it must be noted that not all family-alliance units have such sedentary members.

Leaders *(nakura)* are not chosen through any formal decision, but rather emerge through innate personal qualities. Frequently, but not always, they are among the more sedentary members of the alliance and have some talent in boat-building or fishing or the like, as well as respected characteristics which set them off from their peers. Leadership, however, is as subject to change as is the composition of the unit itself, and different leaders may emerge for the different activities of the unit. For example, ceremonies are led by that person familiar with the proper ritual; fishing activities are led by the man acknowledged as an expert fisherman; boat-building activities may be in the hands of still another man, recognized as a master boat-builder. To add a further complication to this already complicated pattern, all positions are subject to change as the composition of the alliance unit changes.

Social factors provide cohesion to the family-alliance units, whereas work teams are more often formed for economic reasons. Even when intimately involved with a unit over an extended period of time, the nuclear family remains for the most part economically independent of the larger unit. In no sense is the family-alliance unit corporate. A great deal of borrowing and loaning of such essentials as food, water, firewood, betel nut, and cigarettes occurs among the members of a family-alliance unit, but it is all reciprocal. Anyone who borrows from fellow members too consistently without making loans in return will eventually find himself without an alliance unit.

When traveling on fishing trips as an alliance unit, each nuclear family normally fishes independently unless the husband has no one in his family to help him because either his children are too young or his wife has too many demanding duties. In such a case, he may form a work team with one or two adult males of the unit. But, if at all possible, each man prefers to fish alone with other members of his family of procreation, since then he need not divide the catch with others. During these trips, the boats of the alliance unit moor at a central place in the fishing grounds, and some of the members fish in smaller boats away from the anchorage in family groups or work teams, while others, usually older females, remain with the houseboats. All return to the boats at night. If a family does not catch enough fish for immediate consumption, others of the alliance unit give them fish, but surplus catches which are dried and sold in Bongao are the personal property of each nuclear family. Certain types of fishing are more profitably done with several boats, and for these work teams are always formed. At night, if tides and winds are favorable, Bajau practice spear-fishing with kerosene lanterns. For such fishing, nuclear-family units accompany one another, but each in its own boat with its own lantern and claiming its own catch. The additional lights illuminate more fish, to the benefit of all, and the additional persons provide companionship as well as protection from outlaws, who occasionally harass lone Bajau fishermen.

During the day when the men are fishing away from the houseboats, women who have not accompanied their husbands usually scavenge the reefs which are exposed during the low tides. They almost always collect in groups, but whatever each finds is claimed individually and, unless one member is extremely unlucky and finds nothing, no division occurs. The women individually collect firewood in similar groups.

When at one of the five permanent moorages, individual nuclear family units continue to be economically independent of the others. During stays at such moorages, men frequently seek additional income and diversion from fishing, especially if they are not well versed in the fishing techniques of the area, by making boards from trees in the forests. Bajau men always go to the forest in work groups, but, once there, each works individually and claims for himself all boards he cuts. The group provides companionship, as well as occasional assistance, for the individual and allays his fear of traveling alone in the forest.

Boat-building is normally an individual project, but occasionally a man needs assistance to help him over a difficult stage of construction or to provide skills, such as carving, which he does not have. At such times, he calls upon members of the family-alliance unit to form a work team; unless their assistance is needed for a long time, these members expect no payment for their services beyond reciprocal favors. A man with little talent for boat-building, or a young, inexperienced man, sometimes must depend upon members of his alliance unit to construct his entire boat. In this case, the owner provides all materials for the boat and does whatever work he can under the direction of the master boat-builder; in addition, he may be expected to provide sustenance for some of the workers during this period. All depends upon the closeness of the relationship between the men. Most men closely related to the boat-owner would demand no payment, but would certainly feel no qualms about seeking reciprocity from him in a time of their own need. He would, of course, be obligated to give such assistance. On rare occasions, two or three men of an alliance unit may form a work team to construct a boat to sell, in which case profits are equally divided.

Unlike economic activities, Bajau ceremonies usually demand the participation of the entire alliance unit, and sometimes of more distantly related kinsmen. In fact, besides the obvious functions connected with marriage, healing, and initiation, the chief effect of Bajau ceremonies is to congregate the otherwise dispersed Bajau households. Only for ceremonies do large groupings of Bajau houseboats moor at a single moorage.

The simplest Bajau ceremonies are performed alone by the nuclear family. If the family happens to be in the vicinity of the cemetery islands, some members may visit family graves to leave small offerings of betel nut or cigarettes to a recently deceased relative. Sometimes the offering is left out of thoughtfulness for the deceased, but more commonly it is left to insure that his spirit will not visit the living with illness or bad luck. A similar ceremony occurs when a Bajau advertently or inadvertently passes a place known to be the hangout of *saitan* (evil spirits). As a placation for having possibly aroused the displeasure of the saitan by disturbing their home, the trespassers frequently leave offerings of betel or cigarettes or small green or white flags (favorite colors of the spirits). A chant may be recited as the offering is left, but often no formal ritual is involved.

By far the great majority of Bajau ceremonies involve the attendance and participation of an entire alliance unit. Participation frequently extends well beyond the alliance unit, but the unit is most actively involved in the planning and execution of the ceremony. Certain healing ceremonies, which are attended only by members of an alliance unit, are held in response to serious or prolonged illnesses. Members of the unit congregate in the houseboat of the patient while a person familiar with the proper ritual asks the spirits believed to be causing the illness to refrain from their disease-causing activities. Each unit normally has one among its members who is familiar with curing rituals, but, if not, an outsider —almost always a relative—may be asked to conduct the ceremony. The ritual consists of a simple prayer, made in the presence of burning incense to call the spirits, and offerings of food. Several types of curing ceremonies are observed by the Bajau, depending upon the illness, but all initially involve only members of the alliance unit. If the ceremony is the first for the illness, and if the illness is not particularly serious, some members of the unit may feel it unnecessary to attend. However, the more serious the illness—especially the illness of an adult —the more members of the unit attend. And in a case of the critical illness of an adult, all adult members of the unit attend—partly out of real concern for the patient and partly out of fear that, in the event of his death, his spirit may punish those persons who have acted unconcerned with his fate.

One type of Bajau curing ceremony, the *magtimbang* (literally, 'to scale' or 'to weigh'), involves considerably more persons than are in the family-alliance unit, although unit members plan and execute it. In the event of a serious illness, close relatives of the patient may promise the disease-causing spirits to hold a magtimbang if the afflicted is allowed to survive. If the patient recovers, the ceremony is held shortly thereafter. A pole, about twelve feet long, with a sling at either end, is tied at the center to a rope which, in turn, is fastened to a brace erected on the boat for this special purpose. The patient sits in one of the slings, while goods, such as bananas, sugar cane, and firewood, are placed in the other end to balance his weight. The entire pole is then turned several times to the chant of a religious leader and then returned to its original position; the patient is then removed from the sling, and the goods are distributed to the relatives who have attended the ceremony. Although the family-alliance unit of the recovered patient plans the ceremony and contributes to the goods, anyone in the moorage is free to attend, and most relatives of the patient are expected to do so.

The ear-piercing operation performed on all girls, usually during infancy, is normally attended only by the family-alliance unit and other close relatives— siblings or parents of the child's parents. The ceremony probably once had religious significance but now consists only of a minor operation performed by an older person, usually a woman of the alliance unit who is experienced in such matters. An older man familiar with religious lore usually sits in to chant a prayer to insure good luck and health for the child. Almost all female members of the alliance unit attend the ceremony, but most male members, except the father of the child and other adult males of her household, usually do not attend.

The *magislam* ceremony is held for boys when they reach adolescence. The ceremony is patterned after the circumcision of some land-dwelling peoples of Sulu, but the operation involves a mere knicking of the foreskin, incision rather than true circumcision. The celebration may involve only the family-alliance unit, or, if very elaborate, may extend to include additional relatives, or even nonrelatives. If the family is poor or simply does not care to spend the money for an elaborate celebration, the ceremony is a small affair held in the family boat. Persons who are not unit members may attend, such as siblings or first cousins of the boy's parents, and unit members are usually there. Some play music before, during, and after the brief ceremony, while others, especially girls, may dance on the boat, which may be decorated. Both men and women of the unit assist in bathing and dressing the boy. Often, the older man who performs the simple operation is a member of the family-alliance unit; if not, he is a relative of the boy. More elaborate ceremonies include a distribution of rice or sugar, or both, to the entire moorage, with music and dancing on the reef or nearby beach throughout the afternoon and evening hours, during which betel nut and cigarettes are provided to all adult guests. Such elaborate ceremonies may involve considerable cost, and, although the father of the boy is expected to bear the main expense of the celebration, he sometimes will call upon relatives to assist in financing a large celebration. His own and his wife's siblings usually contribute equal shares to the celebration, regardless of whether they are members of his present family-alliance unit, since all probably have been in the past and will be again in the future. All share some of the limelight of the elaborate affair, and all expect reciprocity for their sons' magislams or when they seek a wife for one of their boys. Rarely are contributions asked from relatives more distantly related than siblings of the boy's parents.

A boy depends almost completely upon his kinsmen in obtaining a wife. Even if he should elope and thereby avoid a large brideprice, a settlement nonetheless must be paid which he normally does not have, since whatever money he may have earned is part of the family savings. Because most nuclear families are unable to afford the usual brideprices of 80 to 100 pesos, they must call upon kinsmen —siblings of the boy's parents—to assist. And, even if the boy's family could afford to pay the entire price, tradition would demand that others be asked for some assistance. In one case, the groom's family, being poor, paid less toward the brideprice than any of the other contributors; in another case, the groom's family paid more than 75 percent of the total, with the remainder shared by the eight siblings of the groom's parents. Both cases are unusual, and most fall somewhere between these two extremes. As in all Bajau social and economic relations, reciprocity is the keynote to the event. One always contributes to a brideprice what one has received from that family for a past brideprice or magislam.

Division of the brideprice received by the bride's family follows lines similar to those by which it was collected among the groom's family; that is, it is parceled out to the siblings of the bride's parents, with the parents normally receiving the largest share. Division among the parent's siblings is determined by the amounts they have contributed to past family ceremonies, but, if family quarrels have separated some siblings, they are no longer included in the social activities of the group. It is not unusual for a man to contribute to a brideprice and then a day or so later receive a share, possibly larger than his original contribution, from the same brideprice. This would, of course, be the case if the bride and groom were first cousins; the actual transfer of goods and money usually occurs, even though a good deal of it may return to the donors.

As the preceding discussion reveals, a family with only sons has considerably more expenses than a family with only females; boys require money for both circumcision and marriage, whereas girls have no comparable expenses. The Bajau recognize this disequilibrium, but generally feel that the nearly equal number of males and females in the kin group balances it over time — which it does. But, nonetheless, a family with many sons is a drain on its kinsmen.

Aside from economics, the family-alliance unit has another important function at marriage. It is considered poor taste for the parents of the bride and groom to be directly involved in the sometimes sticky business of coming to an agreement on the brideprice. Consequently, all the negotiation between the two parties is done by siblings of the parents of the bride and groom. Once the boy has indicated his choice for his bride or his family has talked him into marrying a particular girl, adult members of the unit, siblings of his mother or father, or both, visit a houseboat of the future bride's family-alliance unit—never the boat of the future bride. At this time, after they have made their proposal to the family, they leave a gift consisting of family jewelry or other valuables. If the girl's family is interested in the proposal, often after long hours of discussion with the girl's parents and after her own consent, they return the gift to the houseboat of the boy's relatives and announce the price they have decided upon. If they are not interested in the marriage, they ask an unreasonably high brideprice, which the boy's family usually interprets as a rejection of the proposal. But, even if the proposed brideprice is a reasonable one, the boy's family may try to bargain the price down. Eventually an agreement is reached between the two parties, but at no time are the parents of the couple or the bride and groom present at the actual meeting, although the parents do take an active part in the discussions preliminary to the meetings. Once the brideprice has been paid, the marriage can be held. Arrangements for the entire affair are made by the members of the alliance units and other siblings of the prospective parents-in-law. Bride, groom, and their parents continue to have insignificant roles in making the arrangements.

The death of an adult Bajau also demands the participation of the family-alliance unit, as well as any other relatives who may be in the vicinity. After an initial display of grief and mourning by the deceased's alliance unit, the more responsible members conduct the funeral activities. An older person, normally an uncle or older in-law of the deceased (female, if the dead person is female), washes the body and prepares it for burial. Throughout the night following death, a wake is held in honor of the dead man. In the case of an adult death, most adults of the moorage visit the funeral boat during the night to chant prayers and sing mourning songs; if the deceased is a child, normally only close relatives, such as siblings of the parents, attend the wake. The following morning the body is taken to the cemetery islands for burial. The number and composition of the entourage of mourners vary greatly; in an infant's death, only a couple of boats with members of the family-alliance unit may attend, whereas the death of an adult may be mourned by a dozen boats, with relatives of second and third degrees of collaterality also in attendance. As with all Bajau ceremonies, the alliance unit initiates the activities and invites less intimate relatives, or even nonrelatives, to attend the formal ceremony.

Death does not involve a great deal of expense to the survivors, although some outlays of cash are necessary. Most important, a shroud of white cloth must be purchased. Usually, the immediate nuclear family of the deceased has the necessary cash, but, if not, members of the family-alliance unit contribute to the purchase of the cloth. Some families provide food for the mourners who accompany the corpse to the burial islands; in such case, the family-alliance unit makes a contribution, although, if the nuclear family of the deceased is fairly well off, it may pay all the expenses.

Interpersonal relations within the family-alliance unit vary greatly, of course, depending upon the intimacy and duration of the contact between members, the relationships of the members, and individual personality factors. Nonetheless, some generalizations may be made. Normally the sibling tie remains strong even after marriage, although it tends to weaken as one's own children attain adulthood and marriage, to form their own alliance units. Circumstances may separate siblings for months or years, but, even after such separation, the sibling tie may be reactivated. During the early months and years of marriage the sibling tie occasionally overrides the marital bond; I observed many family quarrels in which a spouse sided with a sibling rather than his mate, and, on the other hand, I have heard individuals being chastised by siblings because they have defended mates rather than siblings. However, as the marriage bond lengthens and loyalties are more completely transferred to spouses, the sibling bond weakens. Uninvolved unit members act as mediators in the event of serious quarrels between spouses or other persons of the unit. If differences cannot be resolved, families sometimes break from one unit to join another, either in the same or in a different moorage.

Among the adult members of the alliance unit, patterns of friendship and intimacy follow sex lines; that is, females form close friendships among themselves, as do the males among themselves. Two types of sibling "in-law" relationships are recognized by the Bajau, namely, the relationship between a man and his sibling's spouse or the relationship between a man and his spouse's sibling (the *ipal* relationship), and the relationship between two persons married to siblings (the *bilas* relationship). The nature of the relationship varies greatly among individuals, with the most significant variables, perhaps, being compatibility and the duration of the relationship. Persons who get along and work well together tend to remain in the same alliance unit and work team for long periods of time, perhaps until they break off to form alliances with their own married children. In such cases, intimate relationships develop, which may even override sibling ties on some occasions. Two men who are married to sisters and belong to the same alliance unit over a long period of time develop sentiments and reciprocal relationships not unlike those between siblings. The same is true for men in the ipal relationship, as it is, of course, also for females.

On the other hand, siblings may, for reasons mentioned earlier, form different alliances and never act together in the same unit. Even in such cases, obligations for mutual assistance are always present; but sentiments between siblings often weaken in favor of persons more intimately involved in their everyday lives. Also, family quarrels sometimes separate siblings for years, or even a lifetime.

Relationships among children of an alliance unit are determined by the same variables. First cousins reared within a single alliance unit form almost siblinglike relationships, whereas those who never act together in a single alliance unit feel little intimacy. Illustrative of this is the belief among the Bajau that first cousins who have been intimately reared together are improper marriage-partners, whereas those who have been reared separately may be married without qualms, unless they are patrilineal, parallel cousins.[1]

NOTES

1. Such marriages are believed to be incestuous because cousins in this relationship are considered to be as closely related as siblings. The implication is that children created by the semen of brothers are siblinglike, whereas children born of two sisters or of a brother and sister, are less closely related because females are more passive in conception and merely provide a receptacle for the development of the fetus which is implanted by the male. The prohibition has no significant structural influence on Bajau society, since many such marriages do occur and are legitimized by performing a brief ceremony which includes throwing some object of minor value into the sea.

5. The Localized Kindred

Dakampungan has two meanings among the Bajau. In its most general meaning, it is the totality of ego's relatives, as traced lineally and collaterally through his male and female progenitors—the so-called generalized kindred. But, in a more restricted sense, it means the group of cognatic kinsmen or a group of related family-alliance units who regularly tie up together at a moorage. To avoid confusion, I shall call the first, most general, group a generalized kindred and refer to the second, more restricted, group as a localized kindred.

Theoretically, the generalized kindred could be extended indefinitely to all related persons, and in such a theoretical consideration one could probably speak of all the Tawi-Tawi Bajau as members of one generalized kindred. Such a generalized kindred, of course, never meets as a social group and has little function other than to generate sentiments of obligation and reciprocity among its members, by virtue of their being recognized as kinsmen to one another. Consequently, except as a term for describing the totality of one's relatives, the generalized kindred has little meaning for the Bajau.

The localized kindred, however, is quite a different matter, and the boat-dwelling Bajau of Tawi-Tawi recognize about seven such groups among themselves. Obviously, these localized kindred are not closed kin groups, since every member has kin ties which extend into other groups, either in the same or in a different moorage. And, except for the sedentary core of people found at each Bajau moorage, membership in the groups is constantly changing as families move in and out of the moorage. Each is identified by a headman, or *panglima*, who is considered leader of the groups as well as by the moorage where the majority of its boats are normally found. A single, localized kindred may constitute an entire Bajau moorage, or a moorage may harbor two or three such localized groups.

If a Bajau's mother and father are from different localized kindreds, matters of circumstance usually determine to which he belongs. Or, quite conceivably, he may never find it necessary to state membership in one or the other, but simply use each at his convenience. Most often, though, he comes to identify more closely with one than the other because of the residential preferences of his parents. And, upon marriage he may choose to identify with his wife's localized kindred, which may or may not be different from his own. Two important leads in discovering a Bajau's kin affiliations are his participation in the *maggomboh* ceremony, a first-fruits celebration held during the dry-rice harvest season which theoretically involves all members of a generalized kindred, and the man he recognizes as the headman of the localized kindred.

Bajau kin relationships are vividly demonstrated in the maggomboh (from *omboh,* meaning 'grandparent' or 'ancestor') ceremony which is held each year, usually in July or August. Each household head acquires dry rice from land-dwelling Samal farmers or from other Bajau who raise their own small plots. The rice, having been pounded by the women to remove the husk, is put in a specially made basket which is placed at the bow of the houseboat. That night members of the household sleep with their heads directed toward the rice. The following morning the rice is cooked, molded into a conical shape in a bowl, and taken by family members to a central houseboat, where other relatives have assembled with their own bowls of rice. The bowls—sometimes as many as twenty or thirty—are placed on the deck of the boat, after which a shaman conducts a brief ceremony to call the ancestral spirits to partake of the rice and to bless the living with good luck and health. Taking small portions of rice from each bowl, he mixes them in an empty bowl and offers the combined rice to all the children present. Each family then takes its own bowl of rice home to eat at the next meal. All families do not hold the ceremony on the same day, and any family may participate in any number of ceremonies, so long as they are conducted by relatives. The ceremony serves to reinforce ties among all living kinsmen (not only members of a localized kindred), to remind persons of their deceased kinsmen, and to socialize the children into the kin group. Bajau explain that, if it is not held, illness and death will occur, or great storms with rough seas, strong winds, and heavy rains will visit the area.

If one were somehow able to map out all the maggomboh ceremonies of any one season and the individuals participating in them, he could arrive at the Bajau definition of the generalized kindred. This ceremony emphasizes even distant kinsmen. The ceremony is not limited to the Tawi-Tawi Bajau. Some of these Bajau travel to Sitangkai to participate in the ceremony with kinsmen there, while the Sitangkai Bajau occasionally travel to Tawi-Tawi for the same reason. Similarly, Bajau people living near Semporna, Sabah, participate in some of he Sitangkai ceremonies with people from Tawi-Tawi. Groups participating in the ceremony comprise the *bangsa* (ethnic group) delimited by these Bajau as their own, namely, the Bajau of Tawi-Tawi, Sibutu, and Semporna.

Each localized kindred recognizes a panglima whose chief functions are arbitration and ritual leadership. When disputes cross localized kindred lines, as they may in moorages where there are several such kindreds, the headman of the leading localized kindred of the moorage handles the case. The position of headman ideally passes from father to eldest son, but matters of practicality, such as leadership and wisdom, are more important in determining who holds the position. An old headman in one moorage had several sons, none of whom had leadership abilities and none of whom was interested in the position. At the old headman's death, the eldest son was acknowledged as the headman and was

Two Sitangkai women pound rice for the maggomboh ceremony, in which the many members of their generalized kindred will take part.

addressed by the title, but the position was taken over by the younger brother of the old headman. People gravitated to him because of his natural charisma, and, before long, with no formal decision or announcement, he was recognized as the headman of the group. The eldest son of the deceased headman did not object, because he was not interested in the position. Practical considerations of this sort probably more often determine succession than ideal patterns of inheritance.

The headman ideally settles all disputes in the localized kindred, collects fines, and sometimes solemnizes weddings. In reality, his participation in these events is often minor, although his presence at a dispute seems to give official recognition to the disagreement. He may collect fines from offenders, but often the persons involved refuse to accept his decision and eventually settle the argument among themselves. Any fines which he does succeed in collecting, he usually divides with the offended party. I never saw nor heard of any instance when the decision of the headman was enforced against someone's will. If a man arouses too much antipathy in a moorage, he simply moves on to another and returns after several months have allowed the incident to be forgotten. If a case is particularly difficult, the headman may call in other older men to act as advisers, while serious problems are taken to law-enforcement officials in Bongao; however, the Bajau usually avoid such officials, most of whom they do not trust.

Only in extreme cases is the headman called upon to settle disputes, since most disagreements within a family-alliance unit are settled by the members, themselves. Thus, disputes brought to the headman are usually those which cross alliance units.

The position of headman carries certain social prestige, though not a great deal of wealth. Any wealth a headman may succeed in accumulating is usually through his efforts at fishing or some other such activity, and not through his duties as headman. Frequently, fines are not paid even when levied, and, when they are paid, the normally small amounts must always be divided with the offended party. In general, headmen have very little power, and it would be difficult for them to exert it, even if they so desired. The mobile nature of the scattered individual Bajau families discourages the development of any strong, central political authority. If any headman should become inordinately demanding, in all likelihood, the persons under him would simply move to another moorage and a more tolerant headman.

Title, alone, does not necessarily identify a headman, since the title is often extended to any older man as a term of respect for his age and wisdom. In addition, certain Bajau men have been given appointments as headmen through the office of the sultan in Jolo because of special favors they have done for local politicans. Consequently, any single moorage may have several men who have been appointed at various times as headman, in addition to the traditionally recognized headman. However, these political appointees rarely press their claims, since most do not understand or care about the nature of their appointments.

Besides the headman, each localized kindred has a number of other specialists who perform primarily for members, but whose services may extend beyond the group—especially if their talents have gained some renown. These roles often overlap, however; for example, three headmen in Tawi-Tawi are also recognized as outstanding shamans, and one enjoys local renown as an excellent boat-builder. The *anambar,* a herb-doctor, has knowledge of the use of certain plants in the treatment of wounds, headaches, stomach disorders, and other such ailments. Normally, an ill person is first treated by such a person, but, if the illness persists, then the shaman is called for further treatment. Some shamans are only casual practitioners who rarely perform beyond their own alliance units, whereas others are full-time specialists, who practice even among the land-dwelling Samal and Taosug and enjoy considerable fame throughout Tawi-Tawi. Most shamans fall somewhere between the two extremes. All localized kindred number several shamans among their members who are called upon whenever there is need for their services. Those most closely related are consulted first, but, should the illness persist, a famous, although unrelated, shaman may be consulted. Shamans rarely charge close relatives for the services, although they may charge considerable to nonrelatives—especially non-Bajau. Each family-alliance unit usually has at least one woman who acts as midwife, but, within each localized kindred, several older women are recognized as expert midwives, who are consulted in the event of difficult childbirth. Some men who call themselves *imam* (Islamic ritual leaders) have learned some Arabic chants and are asked to chant at curing ceremonies, funerals, or weddings. Only four such men are found among the Tawi-Tawi Bajau, and they all belong to a single localized kindred. As the Bajau become more Islamic, such men will, no doubt, become more numerous and will achieve greater importance. Most localized kindred also have several men recognized as wood-carvers. These men do the carvings on new boats and on grave markers. Like the shamans, they never charge close relatives for their services, although they usually receive some compensation from distantly related persons and especially from nonkinsmen. Expert boat-builders, too, are frequently called upon by members of their localized kindreds to assist in building or to build an entire boat; except when assisting closely related persons, these men are usually paid for their work.

Although the localized kindred never meets as a group, most of its members come together in the event of an important wedding, curing ceremony, or incision. In no sense is it a corporate group, nor is it a descent group. The meagre property of the Bajau is always held by individuals or individual families; descent is of little importance in Bajau society and is called upon only in selection of a headman, and, as noted earlier, even in this case more practical considerations than lineage come into play.

Members of both the generalized and the localized kindreds are identified by kinship terms that reflect the cognatic principle of organization. Besides generational groupings and consanguinal-affinal groupings, the only persons within the generalized kindred who are distinguished by distinct kin terms are members of the nuclear family. The kin terms which identify them are extended beyond the nuclear family only in very special cases, for example, intimate friendships where nuclear-family kin terms may be used in address or reference. The dispute regarding the degree to which kinship terminology reflects society has yet to be resolved, but the distinctive terms for the nuclear family reflect its basic and independent role in Bajau society. Furthermore, the lack of terminological distinction between father's and mother's relatives is in keeping with the cognatic nature of Bajau society.

Bajau kin terms are a combination of the so-called Eskimo- and Hawaiian-type systems. Ego terminologically distinguishes his mother and father from their siblings, and parents' siblings are called by male and female terms which are extended collaterally to all relatives of their generation. A single term (the same term used for ancestors) is used for all relatives in the second and subsequent ascending generations from ego. Within his own generation, ego distinguishes siblings from cousins and further distinguishes collaterality of counsinship by suffixing "first," "second," "third," and so forth, to the term. Ego's own children are distinguished from nephews and nieces, although the term for nephew or niece is extended to the offspring of anyone in ego's generation. All persons in the second and subsequent descending generations from ego are addressed by a single term. Persons married to ego's spouse's siblings are called by a term which is also extended to include all persons married to kinsmen of ego's spouse's generation.

Persons married to ego's siblings and collateral consanguines of his generation are called by a single term, as are those persons married to ego's consanguines of descending generations (including his own children's spouses). Ego calls all affines in ascending generations by a single term. Excepting the terms for mother and father and uncle and aunt, all Bajau kin terms are neuter; sex may be indicated by adding the proper suffix. An older term, less often used, makes no sexual distinction between mother's and father's collaterals.

Bajau kinship terms are predominantly classificatory. The grandparental and ascending generations are called by a single term. At one time, all members of ego's parents' generation (excluding the parents) were called by a single term; now, division occurs along sex lines. Excluding his own children, all members of the first descending generation from ego are called by a single term, as are all members of the second and descending generations. Affines are lumped even more. A single term describes all affines in ascending generations from ego, while another term describes all affines in descending generations from ego. All affines married to consanguines of ego's generation are called by one term.

6. The Moorage

Although Bajau dwellings are not land-based or sedentary, the Bajau moorages are similar to villages, in that they are places where some Bajau are found all the time, the number depending upon factors discussed earlier.

In each of the five Bajau moorages in Tawi-Tawi, one localized kindred is recognized as the first, or leading, kin group. In most cases, this first group is the one that originally began mooring at the place. Others who began to moor there later recognized the priority of the first group. Tungkalang and Luuk Tulai have two localized kindreds; Tungbangkao has three; while tiny Lioboran and Lamiun have one each. Certain rights and prestige are enjoyed by these "first families." In the event of quarrels, others are often chastized as being outsiders, even though they may have moored there for many years. The headman of the original group is recognized as headman of the moorage, and, although each localized kindred calls upon its own headman for problems within the group, any quarrels which cross group lines are taken to the moorage headman. And should it be necessary for the moorage to be represented at a celebration in a land village, the headman of the first localized kindred would attend.

Lamium illustrates how Bajau moorages are founded. This moorage consists almost exclusively of the married sons and daughters of two brothers and their female first cousin, who began to moor at the place ten years ago after having been frightened from a nearby village of land-dwellers. The moorage is identified among Bajau as the home place of this localized kindred, even though a considerable number of other Bajau have begun to moor there. Eventually, several other localized kindreds will probably emerge at Lamium if the present trend continues, but the founding group will be considered the natives of the moorage, and their headman will continue to be headman of the moorage.

A shift in power occurred between two localized kindreds at Tungkalang. The original localized kindred in that moorage was led by a headman who had enjoyed great renown as a good leader in his younger days. His siblings were equally well known; one was an outstanding magician, another a powerful shaman, another an expert boat-builder, and still another, an excellent fisherman. When I first met the family in 1963, they were living on past laurels, and most were old and somewhat senile. The headman, himself, had only one daughter; one of his brothers had eight children; and the other siblings had only one or two children each. None of the younger generation had the skills or charisma of their parents.

Some four years before my arrival, a localized kindred from a moorage now dispersed had moved to Tungkalang. The adults of the new group were much as the leaders of the old group must have been when they were young—extremely competent in a number of skills, with outstanding abilities in leadership. The new localized kindred, in acknowledgment of the priority of the first group, paid the proper respect to the old headman. At his death they recognized the ascendancy of his oldest nephew to the position. The nephew, unfortunately, was not qualified; he was unlearned in traditional law, had poor judgment, and in general lacked the ingredients of a good leader. After a few rather pathetic cases, it became apparent to the moorage that the man was not a proper headman. No one else in his family fared better than he, so the moorage's inhabitants began to look elsewhere for someone to settle their disputes. The headman of the recently arrived kin group was still faily young—perhaps forty—but well-versed in Bajau tradition and a competent leader of his own localized kindred. Before long, persons began to seek his advice on problems, and, by the time I left the moorage in 1967, he was recognized as the headman of the moorage, and his kin group was considered the leading localized kindred. The older members of the original localized kindred revealed some resentment at the shift in power, but realized that they had failed to provide a competent leader for the moorage. The nephew of the deceased headman continued to act as headman of his localized kindred, but his position of moorage leadership was lost.

In all localized kindreds in the moorage, three different types of households are discernible—namely, sedentary, seminomadic, and nomadic. A nucleus of boats which rarely leave the moorage forms the stable element of the population around which the other boats are clustered. Generally, these households are composed of the immediate family of the moorage headman, married couples of which both are natives of the moorage, families who are predominantly agriculturalists, and those who are involved in some other nonfishing activity. The second group, the seminomads, are usually fishermen whose residence in the moorage is determined by the phases of the moon, or others who, for various reasons discussed earlier, are in the moorage only part-time. The third and smallest group, the nomads, usually moor at the fringes of the moorage and are seldom in any moorage for longer than a couple of weeks at a time. Also included in this last group are those persons passing through the moorage en route to some other destination.

The moorage may be viewed as three concentric circles, the innermost circle being the sedentary population, the second circle the seminomads, and the third the nomads. Overlaying these concentric circles are the localized kindreds. Within these localized-kindred boundaries, the family-alliance units may be considered as a series of smaller circles, not concentric, but overlapping one another and overlaying the three major concentric circles, since a family-alliance unit often consists of sedentary persons, seminomads, and sometimes even nomads. Also, any single member of an alliance unit may at some other time belong to a number of other alliance units in the moorage, conceivably in a different localized kindred. If another dimension is added to the above circles, it is possible to illustrate how the alliance units of one moorage extend to and include members of other moorages, thereby revealing the web of kinship ties which connect the five Tawi-Tawi Bajau moorages.

Ideally, social stratification in a Bajau moorage follows a pyramidal structure which ignores localized-kindred affiliation. At the top of the pyramid is the headman; on the second step are the spritual leaders, the healers, and the magicians; on the third step are the permanent residents of the moorage, followed on the fourth step by the seminomads, and ending on the fifth with the true nomads. However, this stratification is artificial in that it fails to account for the many exceptions. For instance, a seminomadic man, because of his success as a commercial fisherman, may have considerable wealth, which, coupled with a strong personality, may make him one of the most influential persons in the moorage. Similarly, a very old man, although recognized as the moorage headman, may be mostly disregarded by the moorage dwellers because of his senility. Some of the seminomadic commercial fishermen, even though they may be wealthier than some permanent residents of the moorage, may be considered somewhat inferior because of their transitory position in the moorage. Likewise, many an imam or shaman, whose position has high status, leads a seminomadic life. A sense of prestige is rapidly becoming associated with house-living, and a corresponding sense of inferiority, with boat-living. This will, no doubt, be a strong influence in accelerating the move to houses within the next few years as more sea folk embrace house-dwelling.

Only on two occasions do the several localized kindreds of the moorage act as a unit: (1) during a ceremony to rid the moorage of disease-causing spirits, and (2) during a communal fish drive, held most commonly in the Bilatan waters. Although a large wedding celebration may attract the entire moorage to the evening activities, the affair is sponsored by one or two localized kindreds and not the entire moorage; most guests are simply passive observers. The curing ceremony and the fish drive cut across localized-kindred lines and involve active participation and planning by almost all moorage members.

During periods of much illness, death, or unusually bad luck, a ceremony is held to rid the moorage of the evil spirits believed to be causing the misfortune. This probably occurs no more than once or twice a year. Each family contributes a small amount of money or goods toward the construction of a small boat to carry away the trouble: one family may provide a sail, another bamboo outriggers, another food offerings, and so forth. Members of the moorage representing the several localized kindred then construct the boat and place offerings on it. The shamans of the moorage from the several localized kindreds pull the boat through the moorage while chanting to attract the disease-causing spirits. After they have traveled through the moorage waters, the boat is taken to the open sea and set adrift, in the belief that the disease-causing spirits have been attracted to the boat and will drift away from the moorage with it.

The communal fish drives held especially at Tungbangkao also involve the active participation of most members of the moorage as well as any Bajau fisherman who may be fishing nearby. As mentioned, during the neap tides fish are attracted to the Bilatan reefs for feeding. When weather conditions permit—usually about four or five times a year—the moorage men and boys, and sometimes a few women, leave the moorage in as many as a hundred boats to entrap the fish in nets. Certain men, recognized as expert fishermen, act as leaders, and the catch is divided equally among the participants. Although most of the participants are related, kinship in itself is not a prerequisite for joining the drive.

Because of the kinship ties and frequent movement among the moorage members, in many respects all five Tawi-Tawi Bajau moorages represent a single community. Moorages in close proximity naturally have more contacts together than with distant moorages. Frequent—indeed, daily—communication exists between Luuk Tulai and Tungkalang, as well as between Tungkalang and Lamiun, and Tungbangkao and Lioboran. Contacts between the Sanga-Sanga moorages and the Bilatan moorages are less frequent, but, as indicated earlier, the rich fishing grounds and the burial islands attract many of the Sanga-Sanga Bajau to Bilatan. Bajau from Tungbangkao or Lioboran, who have several days' business in Bongao town, generally moor their boats at Tungkalang, since many are afraid of possible maltreatment from the non-Bajau population in Bongao. As a result, Tungkalang often has a large transient population.

The Tawi-Tawi Bajau recognize the Sitangkai Bajau as members of their *bangsa,* or ethnic group, but view the Bajau of Siasi, Jolo, and Zamboanga as a different, albeit closely related, group. Kinship ties verify the Bajau view; many, and significant, kinship ties connect the Tawi-Tawi and Sitangkai Bajau, whereas few and insignificant ties extend northward to Siasi and Jolo.

Part Two

THE HOUSE-DWELLING BAJAU
OF SITANGKAI

7. Habitat

Twenty miles southwest of Tawi-Tawi Island is the Sibutu Island group, home of the most Islamicized Bajau in Sulu. These Bajau, concentrated in the administrative center of Sitangkai, are more closely related to the Tawi-Tawi Bajau through kinship and other cultural features than to any other group of Bajau, excepting perhaps those of Semporna. The scant evidence indicates that the ancestors of the Tawi-Tawi Bajau once lived in their houseboats in the Sibutu Islands. Long before any of the Sibutu Bajau built houses, a small group of Bajau apparently migrated to the Tawi-Tawi Islands, while the remainder continued their boat-dwelling way of life in the Sibutu Islands until twenty-five years ago, when they began to move into houses.

About thirty miles from Borneo, the Sibutu Islands are the southernmost islands in the Republic of the Philippines. Low coral islands unsuited for little agriculture except copra production, all are plagued with perennial shortages of drinking water. Sibutu, the largest island, is only sixteen and one half miles long, with a maximum breadth of two and one half miles, and, except for one hill which rises 448 feet, is only a few feet above sea level. A narrow channel about three miles wide separates Sibutu from Tumindao Island, the second largest island of the group. Other important islands in the area include Sitangkai, the commercial and administrative center of Sibutu; Tanduwak, a tiny island off the southern tip of Sibutu and host to a Bajau village;Siculan, site of the only lighthouse in the islands; Sipangkot, home of a village of land-dwelling Samal; and Omapoi, the northernmost Bajau village in the islands (see Map 3). All the islands of the archipelago are low, only a few hundred yards in extent, and surrounded by reefs which are bared at low tide.

South and west of the islands, extensive reefs support an incredibly rich marine life, to make the Sibutu Islands one of the most lucrative fishing grounds in Sulu —indeed, in all the Philippines. Because of these reefs, most of the waters surrounding the Sibutu Islands are calm and gentle, with an exception in the northern portion of Sibutu Island, which is protected by only a narrow, fringing reef. The extensive reefs make it unnecessary for the Bajau to travel to the open sea for fish, and they are consequently the most confirmed reef-fishermen of all the Sulu Bajau.

Until fairly recent times, the Sibutu Islands were inhabited exclusively by Samal-speakers, who even today probably represent more than 90 percent of the

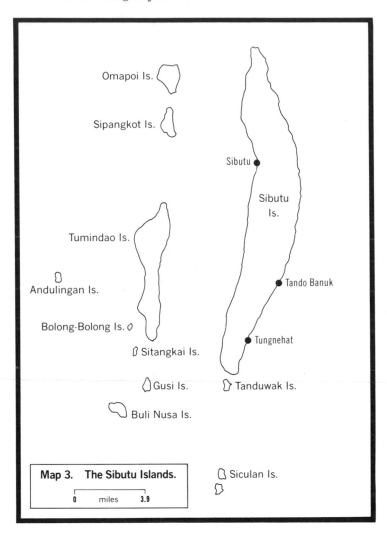

Map 3.   The Sibutu Islands.

0   miles   3.9

population. The remaining 10 percent consists mostly of Taosug, and a few Chinese and northern Filipinos.

The prehistory of the islands is virtually unknown. Earliest written reports of the area are by American administrators who first went to the islands at the turn of this century. The Spaniards never had settlements beyond Bongao, and, although scouting parties doubtless visited the Sibutu Islands, they left no known records of their observations. Consequently, the islands were almost completely bypassed by the mainstreams of Western activity in Southeast Asia until fairly recent years. The first written accounts of the islands mention two groups of people—one living in boats on the sea and one living in houses on the land.

In the early days of this century, flotillas of boat-dwelling Banjau regularly moored at Bolong-Bolong, Andulingan, Omapoi, and Tanduwak, while large communities of land-dwelling Samal were at Sibutu, Tumindao, Tandobanuk, and Tungnehat (see Map 3). Before the recent commercial contacts with the outside world, the two peoples apparently carried on a symbiotic relationship, with the boat-dwellers trading their fish and sea products for the cassava and few fruits of the land-dwellers. Today the traditional specializations persist, although some Bajau have abandoned fishing and some land-dwellers of Sibutu Island have gained renown throughout Sulu as master launch-builders. Besides their different sea and land orientations, religious differences also have traditionally separated the groups: the Bajau continued to follow their native religious practices long after the land people were converted to Islam.

Politically, the islands were a part of the Sulu sultanate and were governed by several hereditary datu directly responsible to the sultan, who ruled locally over village headmen. It is unclear how the Bajau fit into this political structure. The first official Bajau panglima was appointed by the Sultan in about 1920, but before that the datu periodically demanded tribute from the boat-dwelling people. The boat-dwellers were, however, never directly involved in the affairs of the sultanate.

At the beginning of this century, the tiny, uninhabited island of Sitangkai was used as a Bajau burial ground. The nearest Bajau moorage was at Bolong-Bolong, about a mile north, while other Bajau moorages were located at Andulingan, Omapoi, and Tanduwak. According to local lore, some time around 1900, a Chinese man from Borneo, named Bua, visited the Sibutu Islands to investigate the possibility of setting up a small trading store in Sitangkai. Well knowing that the success of his venture depended upon his contacts with the Bajau, Bua cultivated close friendships with the nearby Bolong-Bolong Bajau, as he traded his manufactured goods for their dried fish. His business attracted a few land-dwelling Samal from Sibutu, and, before long, half a dozen houses were strung along the eastern side of Sitangkai Island. Soon the population was further increased as the Bolong-Bolong boat-dwellers began to moor regularly at Sitangkai. More land-dwelling Samal moved to Sitangkai, and more Bajau boats began to moor there, so that by 1905, when the first American administrator arrived in the Sibutu Islands, Sitangkai was regarded as the commercial center of the archipelago, with about twenty-five houses and a sizable flotilla of Bajau houseboats. During the same year, the first mayor of the Sibutu Islands was appointed by the American administration; before that time the islands had been ruled by the old datu under the watchful eye of the United States Army in Bongao. In 1915, the first school was built in Sitangkai, and an American customs officer regularly lived in the settlement. The village continued to attract more Bajau and land-dwelling Samal, as well as a few Taosug families from Jolo. The present wharf was built in the mid-1930s to facilitate the loading and unloading of the interisland steamers, which some years before had made Sitangkai a port of call, to pick up the dried fish of the Chinese fish-buyers. In the late thirties a few flimsy shacks were the first Bajau houses to appear on the reef in front of the emerging Sitangkai settlement. However, with the outbreak of World War II and the establishment of a Japanese outpost at Sitangkai, the Bajau returned to their boats and fled to the more remote islands and reefs, and the Chinese either left the village also, or died at the hands of the Japanese. As a result, Sitangkai almost reverted to its former uninhabited state.

With the cessation of hostilities and the reestablishment of peace, the Bajau and the Chinese merchants returned to Sitangkai. In 1946, an enterprising and imaginative Bajau headman, named Alari, constructed the first permanent Bajau house on the reef a thousand feet in front of the landhouses of Sitangkai. It was an elaborate structure of two stories, with several balconies and ornate carvings throughout, built largely to display the wealth he had somehow managed to accumulate. Within months, another Bajau headman, Alari's rival for leadership among the Sitangkai Bajau, erected an equally impressive edifice a few hundred feet from Alari's original house. Other Bajau began to follow the innovation of their leaders, and within a short time a small village of Bajau houses was clustered in front of the Sitangkai land dwellings. The same Alari apparently learned that house-living per se was not sufficient to qualify him as a respectable member of Sulu society, so a few years after his house-building experiment, he built the first Bajau mosque in Sitangkai. He had planned the mosque project for some time, having in the previous year sent his youngest son to Tawi-Tawi to learn Islamic ritual from an imam who had earlier befriended Alari. With the son's return and with the assistance of friendly land-dwellers of Sitangkai, Alari and his kinsmen began to learn Islam and to throw off the pagan shackles that had marked them as outcasts for centuries. Other house-dwelling Bajau observed the metamorphosis of Alari and his family from outcast pagan boat-dwellers to respectable Muslim house-dwellers and were sufficiently impressed to join the new Islamic Bajau community. The move to houses accelerated with such great speed that by 1963, when I first visited Sitangkai, there were only about thirty families still dwelling in houseboats. In 1966, when I returned for a longer stay, fewer than a dozen families were still clinging to the boat-dwelling life, while more than 2,400 Bajau were living in houses built over the reef.

It is difficult to pinpoint any single reason why the Bajau moved to houses; rather, a series of events, interacting at an appropriate time, seems responsible for the movement. The Bajau were apparently first attracted to Sitangkai by the early Chinese fish-buyers, who offered a ready market for their fish as well as a supply of essential small manufactured items, such as clothing, fishing supplies, matches, and tobacco. Hard upon the heels of the Chinese, American administrators arrived to usher in a period of peace and stability, a rare phenomenon in Sulu, if early sources are to be believed. The northern islands had long been battlefields for countless conflicts between the Spaniards and Muslims, and, even before the arrival of the Spaniards, Sulu history was heavily punctuated with petty wars between datu attempting to usurp one another's power. Add to these hostilities the piracy endemic to the islands for unknown centuries and the occasional slave-raiders from Borneo, still remembered by Bajau old people, and one may glean some notion of the hostilities of the area. Probably this hostility, coupled with their migratory fishing habits, encouraged the Bajau to live in boats away from the more heavily populated areas. With the coming of the Americans and their police powers, Sitangkai became a safe, as well as a convenient, place to live, so Bajau houseboats began regularly to moor there, as they rested from their fishing cycles. The intimate contacts with the house-dwellers, as well as Sitangkai's new cash economy encouraged some Bajau to experiment with house-living and then with Islam. House-living and Islam had always been the hallmarks of their social superiors, and those first few ambitious Bajau who saw in them a way out of their traditional outcast, pagan state grasped the opportunity. Their success spurred others to follow suit, until now, when boat-dwelling pagans have almost vanished from the Sibutu waters.

The Bajau move to houses was not confined to Sitangkai, although it began there. The Bajau at Omapoi have almost completely moved to houses, while at Andulingan and Bolong-Bolong there are no longer villages of any sort, since the boat-dwellers who formerly moored there now live in houses at Sitangkai. Some of the boat-dwellers of Tanduwak built houses there, as others moved up to Tungnehat on the eastern shore of Sibutu, where they constructed houses to form the second largest Bajau community in Sibutu.

Today Sitangkai is a unique spot in the Philippines and is "blessed" with almost everything a village should not have. The island has no drinking water, so all water must be caught during the rains or, during droughts, transported from the brackish wells of Sibutu Island. Two miles of shallow reef water separates the town from the wharf, and all goods must therefore be moved to and from the large ships in small boats. Low tides expose surrounding reefs, which completely isolate the community from sea traffic. And, finally, inadequate, infertile soil on Sitangkai Island discourages any argiculture other than copra production, thereby necessitating the importation of all agricultural products from elsewhere, mostly Tawi-Tawi.

Nonetheless, promoters of tourism have labeled it "the Venice of the Philippines." And, althouth it is not quite Venice, Sitangkai may warrant the appellation. A main canal, the continuation of a shallow channel that cuts through the surrounding reef, roughly divides Sitangkai's 3,400 persons in half. In recent years, walkways of coral rock have been constructed on either side of the canal; two elevated bridges, high enough to allow the passage of small motor launches at high tides, connect the two halves of the village. A large, roofed deck adjoins one of the bridges, to provide Sitangkai's elevated counterpart of the village plaza. On either side of the canal nearby houses are connected by a maze of bridges and boardwalks, while more distant houses are unconnected and must depend upon small boats for access to the main part of town. A few shops are still housed in the original structures built by the Chinese along the island shore, but most are scattered on either side of the canal, having moved to sea to join the rest of Sitangkai's population. The village boasts two mosques, one for the Bajau and one for the non-Bajau, and various branches of a public school, which offers instruc-

The main canal in Sitangkai, lined mostly with shops, serves as a thoroughfare for the villagers in their small boats. The walkways on either side of this important passage are made of coral, rather than the usual wooden slats.

tion through the sixth grade. A small post office and a telegraph office keep the community in touch with the outside world. Some former land-dwellers reveal their terrestrial origins in the small gardens they have planted on man-made islets of coral stone and earth which they have carried from neighboring islands. Others are content with patios of potted plants. A few enterprising individuals, mostly Chinese and non-Bajau, have capitalized on Sitangkai's water shortage by constructing large concrete tanks to store up water during the rainy periods to sell at often phenomenally high prices during the droughts.

Tides govern most activity within the community. At lowest tides it is impossible to move by boat through some sections, while during the highest spring tides, water occasionally spills over some of the eight-feet-high walkways. Fishermen normally leave on the receding morning tide and return on the rising evening tide. Traffic to and from the big boats at the wharf must also await the high tides.

Sitangkai's economy is based almost exclusively upon fishing. In general, the Bajau are fishermen who sell their catches to non-Bajau middlemen—mostly Chinese—who ship them to retail outlets in Mindanao. All the stores and shops are managed by Chinese and other non-Bajau, while most of the nearby cultivable islands are planted in copra by land-Samal.

Sitangkai's regular contact with the outside world is through the two interisland steamers which call weekly from Zamboanga. In addition, unscheduled steamers occasionally call, and several motor launches make frequent trips to Bongao and Semporna in the Darvel Bay of Sabah. Launches regularly move passengers and goods within the island group, but the majority of local movement is still wind- and man-powered.

The Bajau are the largest ethnic group in Sitangkai and represent two-thirds of the population of 3,400. The second largest group is the land-dwelling Samal, followed by the Taosug, the Chinese, and the Christian Filipinos.

The Bajau communities in Sibutu have apparently always been more involved in the political and economic affairs of the land-dwelling Samal than have the Tawi-Tawi Bajau. This is partly related to the larger size of the Sibutu Bajau community. In Sitangkai, they represent about 66 percent of the total population, although this proportion probably falls to about 33 percent when placed in the context of the entire Situbu Islands population. Nonetheless, the number is considerably greater than the mere 4 percent which constitutes the Bajau portion of the Tawi-Tawi population. Thus, in terms of sheer size, the Bajau community in Sibutu could not be ignored by the land-dwelling population. The symbiosis noted between the Tawi-Tawi land-dwellers and sea-dwellers is even more pronounced in Sibutu. This stems partly from the fact that the Sibutu land-dwelling Samal are more confirmed land-dwellers than are most of their Tawi-Tawi kinsmen. The Sibutu Islands are claimed almost exclusively by the land-dwellers, and, even if the Bajau so desired, they could not find land there for agriculture.

The Bajau community in Sibutu has always been more actively involved in the greater political structure of Sulu. Early visitors to the area (such as Taylor) noted that the Bajau owed some sort of ill-defined allegiance to certain land-dwelling datu, who, in return, offered them protection from outside harassment. Old Bajau informants at Sitangkai still recall the early days of this century when they had to pay tribute in dried fish to certain datu. The headman Alari, noted earlier for his important role in initiating the move to houses, was apparently the close friend of a local datu who wanted to gain the political support of the Bajau community. Today, the Bajau represent an importaant voting bloc in Sibutu, and no politician seeking office can ignore them. This is quite a different situation from the one prevailing in Tawi-Tawi, where the small Bajau community is almost completely outside the political community of the islands. Obviously, then, the differences in the sizes of the two Bajau communities are (and apparently always have been) important variables in their relationships with the land-dwelling people.

The Bajau community of Sitangkai is variously acculturated to Islam. Immediate relatives of the Bajau who built the first mosque tend to be the most acculturated, in that they most regularly attend mosque services and three members of their kin group have made the pilgrimage to Mecca. They also tend to live in the central portion of Sitangkai, where many have intimate contacts with non-Bajau. On the other hand, the more recent Bajau arrivals are the least Islamicized, live at the fringes of the village, and have few intimate contacts with non-Bajau. Mosque attendance is an important indication of the degree of Islamicization.

About one-fourth of the Bajau adult male population attends the mosque services fairly regularly, whereas that number is no more than one-fifth among the women. If the men who periodically attend mosque services are added, adult male participation rises to almost one-half, while if comparable females are added, their participation still involves little more than one-fourth of their total population. Virtually all the remaining Bajau claim to be Muslims, but they rarely attend mosque services—some are unfamiliar with the ritual, some claim not to have time, and some are simply not interested. Practically all adults, however, observe and variously participate in certain Muslim life-cycle ceremonies, which some members of all Bajau kin groups have adopted. Most of the ceremonies are not greatly different from those observed by the boat-dwelling Bajau of Tawi-Tawi, except that they reveal the greater influence of Islam in Sitangkai. The younger Bajau, who are more Islamicized, conduct the ceremonies while the older people and less Islamicized younger people observe and assist. Some ceremonies, such as the *magtamat* ceremony held when a youth has mastered certain Koranic chants, are observed only by the most Islamicized Bajau. These ceremonies are not, of course, found among the Tawi-Tawi Bajau, but are universally observed by the Muslim population of Sulu.

Monthly fishing cycles of the Sitangkai Bajau, in general, follow those of the Tawi-Tawi Bajau, except that they are almost completely confined to the surrounding reefs. The communal fish drives, described for the Tungbangkao Bajau, are more popular among the Sitangkai Bajau, largely because the myriad reefs of the area can be most profitably exploited by large groups of fishermen. During the neap tides, flotillas of often well over a hundred boats leave Sitangkai to fish the nearby reefs. During the spring tides of the dark moon, fish are netted by lantern-light in the same manner as in Tawi-Tawi, but, with the waxing of the new moon, a type of seine-net fishing not found in Tawi-Tawi is practiced. The full moon normally demands time away from fishing for ceremonies, but those men who do fish practice net-fishing in nuclear-family units or with one or two male companions. All men, of course, do not always follow these cycles, and many prefer individual net-fishing at all times of the month, but, nonetheless, the above general patterns characterize most Sitangkai fishing.

The Sitangkai Bajau are less mobile than the Tawi-Tawi Bajau, partly because of their house-dwelling and partly because of the proximity of their homes to rich fishing grounds. In addition, they do not have to travel for water, since what water is available in the area is from rain, caught and stored as it flows from the roofs. Nor must they travel for cassava and other food products, which are always available in the Sitangkai market. The occasional trips that the Tawi-Tawi people make to the burial islands are not characteristic of the Sitangkai Bajau, since their dead are buried on their home island. A cemetery located conveniently between Tanduwak and Tungnehat eliminates the same trips for Bajau in those moorages. However, the Omapoi people still use the Sitangkai cemetery and consequently must make periodic visits to it. A trend toward endogamous marriage characterizes the Sitangkai people, who thus have fewer relatives in other Sibutu moorages who must be visited. Some Bajau do, however, regularly visit relatives in the Bajau moorage of Bongau-Bongau, located at the outskirts of Semporna, Sabah, and apparently founded by Sibutu Bajau. Also, many Bajau families periodically return to boat-living for extended fishing trips and when it is necessary to spend several days at wood-working in the Sibutu forests.

But, in general, the Sibutu Bajau are much less mobile than their Tawi-Tawi kinsmen, and some are remarkably sedentary, like the several women I met who, except for brief visits to the very nearby islets, had never left Sitangkai—a far cry from some of the truly nomadic Tawi-Tawi boat-dwellers, who rarely stay in a single place longer than a couple of weeks.

8. The Household

The houses at Sitangkai are, of course, the most glaring difference between this Bajau community and the Bajau communities of Tawi-Tawi. Further inquiry and observation is necessary to uncover the other, more subtle differences between the two groups, but even the most indifferent visitor to Sitangkai cannot help noticing that most of these Bajau are confirmed house-dwellers.

As houses go in Sulu, the Sitangkai houses are well constructed and reflect the general prosperity for which the community is noted throughout the archipelago. All are built on piles driven into the reef floor. Atop these piles, most houses are one-story structures, although the two stories, balconies, and ostentatious carvings of some of the older houses recall a time when families attempted to outdo one another in elaborateness and ornateness. The houses vary greatly in size; older houses tend to be larger—some, 80 feet by 40 feet by 30 feet high at the gable, while some of the more recent ones are only 12 by 20 by 10. Most fall between the two extremes. Except the very poorest houses, all are roofed with corrugated metal, so that the precious rains can be most easily caught and stored for drinking water. Walls and floors are either of commercially-made planks, most of which originate in Zamboanga, or are hand-cut from local trees. Glass windows are nonexistent, but all houses have shutters which are closed during inclement weather and in the nighttime hours. Most houses have extensive, open porches, usually facing to the east, which are used for outdoor household activities, such as drying fish, woodworking, preparing cassava, ceremonies, and children's play. The interior is normally a single room used for daytime activities and for sleeping, while a small house built on the porch serves as kitchen for the household. Bridges connect the house to neighboring houses, which, in turn, are connected to other houses to form the labyrinth of walkways that is Sitangkai. The more seaward houses, however, are often unconnected to their neighboring houses, and their inhabitants must depend upon boats when they visit other parts of the village. Some of the more affluent and aesthetically sensitive have painted

Temporary shacks like these on the outskirts of Liuk Tulai are often the first tentative steps of a boat-dwelling family toward becoming house-dwellers. Such shacks are occupied for the few months of a fishing season and then abandoned.

their houses and keep small verandas of potted flowers; most houses, however, are unpainted and unflowered.

The composition of the Sitangkai household, or *dapaningan* ('a group living in a single dwelling'), reveals considerable differences from the households of the boat-dwelling Bajau. Whereas 77 percent of the boat-dwellers live in single, nuclear-family households, such a composition is found in only 14 percent of the Sitangkai households; all other households in Sitangkai are variations of the extended family. Some of the households are phenomenally large, such as the one-room house I often visited which was home for fifteen nuclear families with a total of forty-six persons. The average, however, is only two or three nuclear families.

As summarized in Table 5, the most common composition of households among the house-dwelling Bajau is based on female relationships, that is, uxorilocality.

TABLE 5. COMPOSITION OF HOUSE-DWELLING BAJAU HOUSEHOLDS.

	number of households
nuclear family	23(14.4%)
uxorilateral extended family	8(5%)
uxorilineal extended family	71(44.4%)
uxorilineal-mixed extended family[1]	10(6.3%)
virilateral extended family	2(1.3%)
virilineal extended family	13(8.1%)
virilateral-mixed extended family	3(1.9%)
virilineal-mixed extended family	7(4.4%)
mixed[2]	23(14.4%)
TOTAL	160

1. A household that is predominantly uxorilineal, with an additional family related through other kin ties.
2. Households from whose composition no dominant pattern emerges.

Fifty-six percent of the Bajau households reveal this organization. The typical household is an uxorilineal extended family of two or three generations in depth —a married couple, their married daughters, and possibly their married granddaughters. The next most common household—16 percent of the total—has a virilocal basis and is typically composed of a married couple, their married sons, and perhaps their married grandsons. Each of the final two types of household, the nuclear family and the mixed, includes 14 percent of the households. Households within the "mixed" category have much variation.

Table 6 reveals that post-marital residence of individual couples, of course, has

TABLE 6. RESIDENTIAL PATTERNS OF HOUSE-DWELLING BAJAU.

type of residence	number of couples
Natolocal village/uxorilocal household	192(65.5%)
Natolocal village/virilocal household	51(17.4%)
Uxorilocal village/uxorilocal household	37(12.6%)
Virilocal village/virilocal household	13(4.4%)
TOTAL	293

the same tendency toward uxorilocality that is found in the composition of households. More than 78 percent of the couples reside uxorilocally, the ideal Bajau residence, exceptions to which are usually based on practical reasons. An elderly couple who had no daughters were quickly approaching the time when they could no longer care for themselves; consequently, their youngest son chose to continue living with them rather than with his wife's family after his marriage. In another case, a wife was orphaned and, rather than live in her deceased mother's uxorilocal household, she chose to live in the household of her husband's parents. Numerous couples leave the wives' parents' households because of quarrels. One young man told me that he and his wife left his wife's household because it was so crowded that they never had privacy for sexual intercourse. The list of exceptions to the ideal of uxorilocal residence could be expanded, but the preceding illustrate the factors which sometimes interfere with the realization of the ideal.

In village residence, natolocality is far more common than other types, as, for example, persons from Sitangkai are more likely to marry one another than they are persons from outside Sitangkai. As could be expected, virilocal village residence occurs the least often.

Perhaps the most dramatic difference between the households of the boat-dwellers and the house-dwellers is in sheer size. However, an examination of the considerations which have contributed to the sizes of households shows that they are not so greatly different from the considerations which determine the boat-dwellers' residence practices. In the first place, the size of the boat-dwelling household is limited by that of the typical houseboat; in most, there simply is not space for more than one nuclear family. And, if the boat is built large enough to accommodate several families, it becomes awkward to maneuver and loses its efficiency in a nomadic fishing culture. Nonetheless, as noted earlier, some houseboats are large enough to house more than one family, and some extended-family households are found among the boat-dwelling Bajau. The more permanent extended-family households are limited to the larger houseboats, whereas those found in small boats are usually emergency adaptations to housing shortages. Thus, the notion of having several related families living together in a single dwelling is certainly not alien to the boat-dwellers.

In many respects, the large, extended households of the Sitangkai Bajau are only a solidification, under one roof, of the fluid family-alliance units of the boat-dwelling Bajau. As noted, except when fishing alone away from the moorage, the Bajau family always joins a larger social unit, composed ideally of siblings of the husband or wife. It is thus a practiced ideal to live intimately with close relatives whenever possible. Consequently, one could predict that, given a more sedentary way of life and larger dwellings, the boat-dwelling Bajau would live in large, extended households. Such, indeed, is what happened when they moved into houses at Sitangkai. Another, very practical, consideration voiced by many Bajau when asked why they prefer to live in extended-family households is that if each family lived in a separate house, the house would be vacant several months of the year as the family followed the monthly fishing cycles. As it is, with several families in one dwelling, the house is always occupied by some families while others are away for fishing or wood-working.

The pronounced uxorilocality found at Sitangkai also has its genesis among the boat-dwellers. As noted, uxorilocality is an ideal among them. A survey among the boat-dwellers revealed that more than 80 percent maintained that a couple *should* have uxorilocal residence, even though more practical problems connected with fishing cycles and other necessary movements discouraged such residence. It appears that when the Sitangkai Bajau were faced with the prospect of sedentary residence in one household, the ideal of uxorilocality came into play. As a result, almost 80 percent of the Sitangkai couples reside uxorilocally. Another factor reinforcing uxorilocality is the fact that Sitangkai men commonly fish in male groups, rather than with their wives as the Tawi-Tawi Bajau do. If women are to be separated periodically from their husbands to reside in an extended household, they will be most compatible and comfortable with their own female siblings. This, too, was remarked upon by many Bajau informants.

The preponderance of natolocal village residence at Sitangkai is due primarily to the large concentration of Bajau in Sitangkai, as well as to their more sedentary way of life. Although the boat-dwelling Bajau claims that it is best to marry a well-known girl from his own moorage, sometimes a youth cannot find a suitable bride among the few unmarried girls in the small moorage he claims as home and consequently must look beyond the intimate circle of acquaintances. His search for a bride is facilitated by his frequent travels, during which he is able to meet many girls in different moorages—meetings which not uncommonly blossom into romance and eventual marriage. In this respect, his contacts are much more dispersed than his more sedentary house-dwelling counterpart in Sitangkai. But the Sitangkai youth has less trouble finding a marriage-partner in his own community, since a large number of unmarried girls is readily available. Thus the trend toward village endogamy.

Like the boat-dwelling Bajau of Tawi-Tawi, the Sitangkai Bajau believe that it is best to marry relatives; however, notions about the best type of relationship differ between the two groups. The boat-dwellers' disapproval of patrilateral-parallel-cousin marriage has been extended to all first-cousin marriage among the more Islamicized Sitangkai Bajau (see Chapter 1, note 2). The recentness of this disapproval reveals itself in that most of the first-cousin marriages in Table 7 are

TABLE 7. MARRIAGE PATTERNS AMONG HOUSE-DWELLING BAJAU.

relationship	number of couples
patrilateral parallel first cousins	14(3.5%)
matrilateral parallel first cousins	6(1.5%)
cross-cousins	10(2.5%)
second cousins	59(14.75%)
third cousins	27(6.75%)
fourth cousins	2(0.5%)
second kamanakan	16(4%)
related, but exact relationship unknown	40(10%)
distant relationship	136(34%)
unrelated	90(22.5%)
TOTAL	400

older couples or ones least acculturated to Islam. First-cousin marriage, except between patrilateral parallel cousins, is still fairly common among the less acculturated Bajau. And the fact that 77.5 percent of all married couples in Sitangkai are relatives indicates that the house-dwellers, like their boat-dwelling kinsmen, still prefer to marry relatives. Indeed, because of the complex web of kinship ties in Sitangkai, it would probably be difficult to find many potential marriage-partners who were not kinsmen.

As noted in the Introduction, the emerging prohibition against first-cousin marriage among the Sitangkai Bajau cannot be adequately explained as acculturation to the land-dwellers' disapproval of such marriages. Rather, it has direct antecedents in the boat-dwelling society. Among the boat-dwellers, marriage between patrilateral parallel cousins is considered incestuous, as is marriage between any first cousins who have been raised together intimately or who have been nursed by the same woman. The same prohibitions have been retained by the house-dwellers, and, because of the large, extended households of the Sitangkai Bajau, the number of first cousins raised together intimately in the same households (who are thereby improper marriage-partners) has been greatly increased. Add to the household mates those first cousins living in neighboring households who intimately interact with one another, and few first cousins remain suitable marriage-partners by traditional Bajau norms. Acculturation to the land-dwellers' prohibitions against first-cousin marriage adds a tinge of disapproval to marriage between those few first cousins who would otherwise be approved marriage-partners. The combination of all these factors will probably eliminate all first-cousin marriage within a couple of generations, if present trends continue.

Although Sitangkai Bajau couples most commonly share a dwelling with several other nuclear families, the family unit has retained much of the individualism and independence found among the boat-dwellers. At marriage, the young husband and wife typically spend the first few weeks moving between the two parental households and eventually settle as part of the wife's uxorilocal household. During these early months, whatever money the husband earns is normally handed over to his mother-in-law, who keeps it with other savings to be used for family expenses. Also at this time the newlyweds eat with the wife's family and, in general, are economically dependent upon it. However, as the husband establishes himself as a bread-winner and when the marriage stabilizes with the birth of a child, the young couple tends to break economic ties with the wife's parents and begins to keep its earnings separate. Like the other nuclear families in the house, they acquire their own cooking utensils, buy their own food, and eat separately from the other families. Whatever equipment the husband may acquire, such as a boat, an outboard motor, or fishing gear, becomes his personal property. In short, despite its membership in a large, extended household, the nuclear family at Sitangkai is almost as independent as its boat-dwelling counterpart in Tawi-Tawi.

During the early months of marriage, separations are common and frequently develop into divorces. Some problems are due to incompatible personalities, since many couples are not well acquainted before marriage. More often, disputes

develop between the newlywed husband and his in-laws. In the event of disagreements between the newlywed and his spouse, members of the household, of
course, always side with their kinswoman. Many Bajau, especially young men,
often spoke of the intolerable loneliness they felt during the early months in their
new households. The birth of a child, however, tends to bridge the emotional gap
between the newcomer and the rest of the household.

In the event of immediate divorce, the portion of the brideprice not spent on
the wedding is refunded to the groom's family. The later the divorce, the less
brideprice is returned; rarely is any returned if the marriage lasts longer than a
year. What property the couple may have accumulated is divided between them,
with household items going to the wife and fishing equipment and boats to the
husband. Children most commonly stay with the wife, although some may go
with the husband and in rare cases the husband may take them all. As among
the Tawi-Tawi boat-dwellers, the spouse responsible for the divorce must pay the
fee to the headman; if both press the divorce, the cost is equally divided.

TABLE 8. DIVORCE PATTERNS AMONG HOUSE-DWELLING BAJAU.

number of divorces	number of married men	number of married women
0	338 (82.3%)	322 (77.2%)
1	60 (14.6%)	82 (19.7%)
2	12 (2.9%)	11 (2.6%)
3	1 (0.2%)	2 (0.5%)
TOTAL	411	417

As indicated in Table 8, the divorce-rate in Sitangkai is higher among women
than men. This may be partly accounted for by the fact that some of the formerly
married young men have migrated to Semporna in search of work and that some
men who previously lived uxorilocally with Sitangkai wives have returned to their
home villages since their divorces.

The greater frequency of divorce in Sitangkai appears to be related to house-
dwelling, or, more specifically, to the extended-family households. Upon marriage, a young couple resides in an extended-family household, most typically an
uxorilocal household. Frequently, the young husband and wife have not known
each other well before marriage and one of them is living in the household as an
outsider. Whenever disagreements arise, little mutual love or attraction exists to
override them, and the members of the household, of course, always side with
their kinsman. As a result, early marriage is a very brittle period, which not
uncommonly ends in divorce. The pattern is different among the boat-dwellers.
As soon as possible after marriage the new couple is expected to have its own
household in which it faces its marital problems alone. Because of the smaller size

of the Tawi-Tawi Bajau population, rarely are a young husband and wife strangers at marriage. And because they live alone in their own houseboat, moving between the relatives of each other, they do not have continual residence with one group of in-laws, with their accompanying interference. I have no data to suggest that boat-dwelling couples who live in joint-family households divorce more frequently, nor would I necessarily expect such to be the case, since the two- or three-family households of the boat-dwellers are usually temporary arrangements and are hardly comparable to the permanent joint households of five, six, or even ten families found in Sitangkai. However, the sentiments that lead to divorce among the house-dwellers are found among the boat-dwellers, namely, that a Bajau is expected to be loyal to kinsmen in the event of quarrels and conflicts which involve nonkinsmen, even spouses. And this is indeed usually the case in the early months of marriage before loyalties have been transferred from kinsmen to spouses. And since the large households of Sitangkai appear to generate such conflict, it should not be surprising to find more divorce among the house-dwelling Bajau.

In no sense is the Sitangkai household a corporate group, but rather each family is an economically independent unit, as are those among the boat-dwellers. On rare occassions, brothers-in-law may decide to buy an outboard motor or fishing nets together, but far more commonly such items are owned individually. Men of a household may fish together, but their catches are always equally divided and are claimed individually. Household members usually share a water-storage tank, but in the event of drought, when water must be purchased, each family purchases and consumes its own. Each family has an area of the house where its daytime activities are localized and where it sleeps on mats at night.

In the larger households, rarely do all members reside in the house at a single time, except during important ceremonies of the household, such as weddings, incisions, or healing ceremonies, which all members are expected to attend. More commonly, two or three of the nuclear families are away on fishing trips or perhaps temporarily residing near Sibutu Island while engaged in wood-working. For some of the more confirmed fishing families, the house is simply a place to live while resting from fishing activities; for others, however, especially the most acculturated, it is their permanent residence, from which they seldom, if ever, return to boat-living.

Although each nuclear family functions independently as an economic unit, some household activities are performed in work groups. Females of the household always assist one another in any work that requires more than individual effort, such as the preparation of cassava or the initial stages of mat-making. Those women who collect from the reefs or who seek firewood on nearby beaches always do so in household groups. Less consistently, men also work as household units. Some men always work and fish with other household males, whereas others prefer to fish with siblings who live in different households. However, group work directly connected with the household is always done by male members as a group. In general, the sphere of male activity and contacts outside the household is much greater than that of the females; some women rarely leave their neighborhoods, whereas men leave daily for work, to visit relatives, or to attend ceremonies.

One man of the household is usually regarded as owner of the house; in many cases he is the one who actually built the original structure or who contributed the major finances toward its construction. Most often he is the eldest male member of the household, although house ownership reveals much variation. Each family living in the house contributes to whatever repairs need to be made on the dwelling. In the case of the older houses, which tend to be the largest in physical size and household membership, the dwelling is regarded as the joint property of the inhabitants, consanguineal relatives of the original owner, who in most cases has now died. At the demise of the owner, the house passes on to the other residents, ideally the owner's married daughters and granddaughters.

The house-owner is usually also recognized as the head of the household group. Matters of a household nature are handled by him; he mediates in quarrels, organizes household ceremonies, instigates household repairs, and represents the household to the rest of the community. In general, his function is not greatly different from the leader of a family-alliance unit of the Tawi-Tawi boat-dwellers.

The extended-family household of the Sitangkai Bajau has tended to break down some of the intimacy characteristic of the boat-dwelling nuclear family. Except for occasional fishing trips for some families, the nuclear family never lives apart from other household members. The ties between sisters and between mothers and daughters are never severed and often override those between husband and wife. On the other hand, husband and wife have less opportunity to develop extreme dependence upon one another. Similarily, because siblings almost always share a household with first cousins and a neighborhood with less closely related persons, their ties to one another are less strong than are those among their boat-dwelling counterparts.

The most intimate and enduring ties within the household are among the female members, excepting, of course, those households which are not based on an uxorilocal axis. In most cases, sisters are raised together as children and continue to live together as married adults until their deaths. Conversely, adult male members of a household have usually come from outside, and boys born into the household know that at marriage they probably will leave for residence in their respective brides' homes. It should not be surprising, then, to discover that sentiments between brothers, as well as between brothers and sisters, tend to weaken and sometimes almost disappear after marriage. Exceptions, of course, occur when married brothers and sisters continue to live in a single household and when married brothers continue to fish and work together, even though they dwell in different households. On the other hand, the intimacy and sentiments men once shared with brothers are often transferred to their brothers-in-law, the husbands of their wives' sisters, who also live in the uxorilocal household. All in all, adult relationships are not greatly different from those found among the boat-dwellers.

Children are most commonly disciplined by their parents, but, in the absence or indifference of a parent, an aunt, uncle, or grandparent disciplines them. Children who attend school are frequently left with other members of the household while their parents spend a week or so fishing away from the household. As a result, all adults in the household, at one time or another, act in the parental role toward the child. Ties of affection between children who have grown up in the same household, that is, between first cousins, are as strong as and sometimes stronger than those between siblings.

A change in kinship terminology among the Sitangkai Bajau appears to reflect the change in household composition. In general, terms for the nuclear family have been extended collaterally in both reference and address. The term for mother may also include mother's sisters and father's sisters; similarly, the term for father has been extended to mother's brothers and father's brothers. *Sibling* includes first cousins, while the term for child or offspring may also mean 'nephew' and 'niece.' Grandfather and grandmother are often called, literally, 'big father' and 'big mother.' The terms of endearment used for siblings and offspring (*otoh* and *arung*) have similarly been extended collaterally.

These changes appear to be related to the extended-family households, especially in light of the fact that the extension of the terms is made only to those kinsmen with whom one lives intimately. Traditional terms are retained for kinsmen with whom one interacts less intimately. If pressed to define a relationship, a Bajau always falls back on the traditional terms, and, for some kinsmen in these categories with whom he is less familiar, he always uses the traditional terms for both reference and address. Thus, the nuclear-family terms are most often extended to members of a household or close neighbors.

This change toward a more classificatory kinship terminology at Sitangkai is not without precedence in the boat-dwelling society. Among the boat-dwellers, the greatest indication of intimacy between two persons is the extension of nuclear-family kinship terms to one another. Most often these terms are used between two men—two brothers-in-law, or perhaps two first cousins, who regularly work together and refer to one another by the sibling term. The nuclear-family terms are less often extended to other relationships, but, when they are, they reveal an intimacy between the two persons which is greater than their biological relationship normally would warrant. Such relationships usually develop after a long period of intimate living and working together. Given this practice among the nomadic boat-dwellers, it should come as no great surprise to discover that when several Bajau families live together in a single household, terms of the nuclear family are extended to other members to reflect this intimacy. Aunts become "mothers," uncles become "fathers," cousins become "siblings," nieces become "daughters," and nephews become "sons." The more common extension of these terms by the Sitangkai Bajau directly reflects the more intimate and enduring ties that characterize most of their social groupings.

If a Sitangkai Bajau dies, his widow and children are usually cared for by the other members of the household, and, because of the large size of many households, their support is no great burden to any single family. Nonetheless, a young widow expects, and is expected, to remarry after a proper period of mourning—usually about a year. In the case of a wife's death, her husband less commonly remains in the household, but rather returns to his natal household. Whether or not his children accompany him depends upon a number of factors. If the children are older, they frequently prefer to stay in their mother's household, or if the father's household has no one to care for them or is already overcrowded, the children may remain in their mother's household. If the father or his deceased wife has childless married siblings, the children may be adopted by them. I encountered four widowers who married either their wives' sisters or first cousins and thereby continued to live in the same households. This would seemingly be the best solution, but is not, of course, always feasible.

As households become excessively large and crowded, they tend to segment. Most often this segmentation occurs when a child or two of a nuclear-family unit attempts to continue to live in the household after marriage; the cramped quarters encourage the newlyweds and the parental family to form their own household. Quarrels among household members also account for some segmentation. When such segmentation does occur, the new house is usually built near the parent house. As a result, the entire Bajau section of Sitangkai can be blocked off into kin neighborhoods. The same sort of segmentation has been described for the sibling-alliance units of the boat-dwelling Bajau, but, because of their nomadic movements, neighborhoods do not develop among them.

A definite trend toward smaller households is evident at Sitangkai. The first Bajau houses were large structures built by the three headmen of the three kindreds then residing at Sitangkai. These three houses are still the largest in Sitangkai and have the largest memberships. They were apparently built large in order to display the wealth of the families, as well as to serve as family meeting halls where all the boat-dwelling kinsmen could rest from fishing activities and attend ceremonies. The houses still partly serve these functions. Later houses have been smaller, since they are not needed as family meeting places, but rather only to house a few nuclear families. The most recent houses, especially those of the most acculturated Bajau, are even smaller and are obviously intended to house only one nuclear family, which many of them do. Most of the young, acculturated couples desire their own houses and often mentioned the difficulties of living in households run by the traditional notions of the older members. The trend toward single-family households, actually a return to the boat-dwelling pattern, appears to have been partly influenced by the land-dwelling people, who typically live in nuclear-family households. Equally contributive is the greater wealth enjoyed by the present generation of Bajau—wealth which may be displayed in individual family homes.

9. The Neighborhood and Work Teams

If things were as the Bajau profess them to be, each household in Sitangkai would be uxorilocal and surrounded by other households related to one another through female kin ties. And, although this seems to be the case at first glance, the reality of residence patterns rarely adheres to this ideal. The Bajau neighborhood often has a preponderance of related uxorilocal households, but in all neighborhoods the uxorilocal ideal gives way to more practical considerations—not greatly different from those which account for the deviance from the ideal of uxorilocal household composition. Nonetheless, the houses comprising a neighborhood—usually four or five—are closely related, although the genealogical relationship has considerable variation. The houses are physically near one another, and the neighborhood is often identified by the name of the man who most commonly acts as its leader.

In contrast to Sitangkai, the boat-dwellers' neighborhood is a fairly insignificant social unit and may be said to exist only in that family-alliance units tend rather consistently to moor their houseboats in the same part of the moorage near other family-alliance units, which they recognize as being more closely related to them than other units of the moorage. Interaction between the units, however, is at a minimum, except for occasional large ceremonies and the rare communal fish drives at some of the moorages. And since members of the units are constantly moving in and out, little opportunity exists to develop intimacy beyond one's own alliance unit. In many ways, the Sitangkai neighborhood is only a crystalization of the clusters of related family-alliance units found in the boat moorages. The family-alliance unit has become a household, and the several family-alliance units have become a neighborhood; however, because of the sedentary life of these people, the neighborhood is a permanent social grouping, with enduring social ties that intensify the ties of kinship which unite the several households. And, of course, as noted, the Sitangkai neighborhoods are predominantly uxorilocal.

An examination of twenty-two Sitangkai neighborhoods, constituting slightly over half the Bajau neighborhoods in Sitangkai, reveals several structural types. Only two have an exclusively uxorilocal organization, nine are predominantly uxorilocal with various exceptional individual households, three are predominantly virilocal with individual household exceptions, and the remaining eight reveal no dominant pattern of organization. Sizes of neighborhoods range from three to eight houses with an average of five, or from sixteen to seventy-four persons with an average of forty-six. The households are usually, but not always, connected by bridges. Adult members visit back and forth freely, and work groups and ceremonies which extend beyond a household are often composed of neighbors. The neighborhood, also, of course, includes children's play groups.

Even though households within a neighborhood are related and generally interact with one another more frequently than with households outside the neighborhood, they are in no sense isolated social islands within the Bajau community. Each household has members who have left the household, and often the neighborhood, for marriage, and each, of course, has members who have married into it from outside that neighborhood. These members who marry outside or into each household relate it to other neighborhoods in the Bajau community with whose members they form work and ceremonial alliances.

Variation is the keynote in the structure of all Bajau alliance groups, but, nonetheless, certain common features may be abstracted. In the case of work alliances, compatibility is the most important criterion for membership; the men must get along well to work together, and, if they do not, they simply do not form alliances. Other criteria for membership include acculturation to Islam, occupational preferences, age, and, of course, sex. Men acculturated to Islam choose to work with other acculturated men. Obviously, only persons who work at the same occupation form work groups. Age is important in that the work of certain work groups demands able-bodied men and is too strenuous for older men. On the other hand, ceremonial action groups usually recruit older, more learned men. And because of the nature of the work, most groups, excepting some ceremonial groups, exclude members of the opposite sex.

Ideally, one works with his siblings or his parent or other members of his natal household, if they meet the above criteria, since these are the persons who can always be trusted and with whom one has learned to work. If for some reason these people are not available, one works with one's household mates (if they are different from those mentioned before)—often because of the convenience of the alliance, the trust and intimacy that develops between members of a household, and common interests. If additional men are needed, members are recruited from the neighborhood of one's own household or one's affinal household—again, because kinsmen are the most dependable and trustworthy. In all work teams, the closer the relationship of the two men, the better; if closely related persons are not available, then one looks further in the kinship field, or even beyond the kinship field.

Compatibility is less important in ceremonial work teams, although persons openly hostile to each other avoid actively participating in the same ceremony. A core of closely related kinsmen, often composed of members of work teams, forms the nucleus of every Bajau ceremony. If additional participants are desired, invitations are extended further into the kin field, or even to nonkinsmen. Peripheral guests at the larger ceremonies—weddings or incisions—may include even non-Bajau.

Women's work teams are fewer and display less variation than the male alliances. Work teams always consist of persons from the household or the neighborhood. Women attend ceremonies away from the household less commonly than men, and, when they do, the ceremonies are usually those of siblings or siblings-in-law. They rarely participate actively in ceremonies, but rather assist other females in preparing food for those occasions.

Male members of a common household may regularly work together in a work team, or they may each more frequently establish alliances beyond the household. And, although two men may work more often with one another than with anyone else, they sometimes form alliances with other men for different activities.

The similarities between this land-dwelling household group and the boat-dwellers' family-alliance unit should be apparent. Membership in both groups is usually based on consanguineal or affinal sibling relationships, or on the most immediate extension of these relationships. And, although both the Tawi-Tawi and Sitangkai Bajau tend to work fairly regularly in groups with two or three other persons, they both periodically change alliances when they engage in different activities. In general, Sitangkai women more consistently work in the same work teams and range afield less than the men. And upon closer examination, further distinguishing features are seen to differentiate the Sitangkai work and ceremonial teams from those of the Tawi-Tawi Bajau.

Less acculturated Bajau tend to fish with their wives, whereas the more acculturated fish with other males, their wives having accepted the land-dwellers' notion that fishing is unfit work for women. The type of gill-net fishing most frequently practiced by the Bajau can efficiently be done by two or three persons, so most fishing alliances between men consist of these small groups. The composition of these groups varies greatly. In some cases, men married to sisters in a common household fish together exclusively, whereas other men in a similar household situation may all have fishing partners from outside the household, and even outside the neighborhood. Obviously, personal factors determine each case.

If a man who has no other fishing partner enters a household that has only one other adult male, he most likely will fish rather consistently with that man unless the two personalities prove incompatible. Quite often the newly arrived man discovers that the other household men already have fishing alliances. He has the alternative of either joining one of the household work teams or continuing his fishing habits with his own male kinsmen. Frequently in the early months, and even years, of marriage, a man does the latter. As his ties in his wife's household become stronger and more intimate, he may dissolve the alliance with his consanguines in favor of his affines. Or he may continue to fish with his own kinsmen until such time as he begins to fish with his son or sons-in-law. Men who continue to live in their parental households after marriage, of course, continue to fish with the other males of the household. Frequently, men from other households of the neighborhood prove more compatible as fishing companions; often these are men who fished together before marriage and who married into the same neighborhood. Whatever the relationship, it rarely extends beyond the first degree of collaterality, affinal or consanguinal, and most commonly is a sibling-sibling,

A Bajau mother and daughter of Sitangkai mend the nets while the men of the household are out fishing.

sibling-in-law-sibling-in-law, father-son, or father-in-law-son-in-law relationship.

Other types of fishing practiced in the Sitangkai waters demand more participants than the two or three persons usually involved in gill-net fishing. Among these is the so-called *magsauk,* or seine-net, fishing practiced during the periods of no moon and new moon. Anywhere from four to eight boats, each usually with two men, participate in magsauk fishing. After arriving at a promising fishing spot, the large net is submerged between two boats. Other participating boats leave with lighted lanterns to attract schools of fish which they then direct over the seine net. After all lanterns have returned and a sizable school of fish is above the net, dynamite is exploded and the stunned fish are raised in the net. The fish are scooped up in five-gallon tins and are equally divided among the participants. The net and dynamite used in this type of fishing are usually owned by one man, who acts as leader. At dawn, the boats all return to Sitangkai and take their catches to the fish-buyer regularly patronized by the net-owner. The net-owner gets about one-fourth of the price received for each of the participants' tins as his payment for furnishing the net and dynamite. In addition, he, of course, receives payment from the fish-buyer for his own share of the catch. The crews are usually organized along kin lines. The fishermen of each boat are usually men who regularly fish together with gill-nets; thus the group is simply a collection of the boat crews discussed previously. Although the majority of a magsauk crew is often drawn from a single neighborhood, there are usually some nonneighborhood men, related in varying ways to members of the neighborhood.

Another type of net fishing, the *sinsoro,* also demands the efforts of a group of fishermen. This method may be practiced either night or day. Once a school of fish is spotted, it is surrounded by the large nylon mesh net, which is then pulled to the boat with the entrapped fish. The net itself is usually owned by one man, who receives the largest share of the catch. Sinsoro fishing demands no more than two or three boats, and, like the magsauk crews, these crews are simply combinations of the gill-net crews and are frequently neighborhood-based.

The second most important male work teams in Sitangkai are those of the stevedores. A few stevedores also fish, but most find stevedoring a full-time job that provides a sufficient income. Ten merchants in Sitangkai regularly employ crews of stevedores to transport their merchandise to and from the interisland steamers that call at the wharf. Crews range from three to six members, with an average of five. They are paid a fixed price for each item—tins of fish, crates of dried fish, bags of copra, cases of soft drinks—that is moved to and from the wharf. Each crew has a leader who coordinates activities with the merchant and the ship's captain. He and the merchant both keep account of all items transferred, and after each ship leaves, they compare notes; once a month the merchant pays the leader, who, in turn, divides the cash equally among his fellow crew members. Other than prestige, the leader receives no additional compensation for his extra duties as leader. The only requirement for the position, besides personal leadership, is literacy, since he must keep account of the cargo.

Like other work teams, the stevedore crews display much individual structural variation. They usually consist of kinsmen, such as brothers, fathers, first cousins, and the affinal counterparts. Only one of the ten crews is composed exclusively of members of a single household; members of three of the crews are all from different households—one represents a single neighborhood, and each of the remaining two represents two neighborhoods; the other crews have members who represent from two to five households, distributed among two to four neighborhoods.

Other work teams are formed to make wooden boxes which are sold to the Chinese fish-buyers, who use them for packing dried fish for shipment. Box-making work teams take two forms, a large flotilla of related persons and smaller groups of workers. A large group of related families, sometimes as many as twenty couples, periodically leaves Sitangkai for several days of houseboat-living near the forests of Sibutu Island. During the daytime the women do enough fishing and collecting to keep the family in fish, while the men go to the forests in groups of three or four to fell trees which they cut into boards. After a sizable number of boards has been cut, the flotilla returns to Sitangkai, where each man makes boxes to sell to the resident fish-buyer. The flotillas reveal no consistent structural type; the majority of the members are usually from one neighborhood, and the nonneighbors who join are often related in some fashion. However, some unrelated houseboats sometimes join a flotilla, rather than mooring alone. The flotilla convenes largely for companionship, whereas the male work groups are utilitarian, in that members assist one another in the tedious business of felling and splitting trees. These work teams reveal the same familiar varied structure of other Bajau work teams.

Six Bajau men who own motor launches regularly employ small crews. These crews range from two to four members, are kin-based, and are structurally similar to other Bajau work teams. Members of two of the crews are all from different households; members of one crew are all from the same household; while the remaining three represent two and three different households, each. One man, the owner of the launch, acts as captain. Usually several other persons, variously related to the crew, accompany the launch, but they are not regular crew members and always have some other occupation at which they work more consistently.

A few Bajau who are engaged in small-time smuggling between Semporna and Sitangkai constitute three work teams. All of these men are from the most acculturated segment of Sitangkai and, because of their profession, are among the wealthiest and most respected members of the community.[1] One distinctive feature of these smugglers' work teams is the closeness of the relationship of the men, a feature possibly explainable by the fact that, since smuggling is illegal, it is best to work with persons such as siblings, whom one can always trust. One unit consists of a father and his two married sons; another, two married brothers and the husband of their sister; and the third, three married brothers. No members of any of the groups share a household. Again, one man usually acts as leader and is responsible for making the Borneo contacts for buying and the Sulu contacts for selling.

Female work teams are considerably fewer and simpler than those of the men. The women who occasionally fish always do so with their husbands, or, if they are widowed or divorced, with a brother or father from their household. Women who collect from the reef or gather firewood from the beaches usually do so with other household women and children. Few other duties take women away from the house. When household chores require assistance, other female members are readily available. In the larger households, women, of course, form closer relationships with some members than with others and more consistently work with them. In the event of a ceremony which involves neighborhood participation, neighboring women assist women of the sponsoring household in preparing food, playing music, and decorating the house.

As noted previously, few Bajau ceremonies involve the participation of only the members of a single household. Perhaps the simplest of all Bajau ceremonies is when a lone individual, or one with one or two housemates, leaves a small offering of betel or cigarettes for a deceased relative at the graveside, followed by a short prayer. All other ceremonies demand attendance by most adult members of the household, as well as persons from outside the household, and even the neighborhood.

The simplest of the curing ceremonies, usually the first stage of treatment for any illness, involves only a handful of persons. Rarely do all household members attend such a ceremony, but two or three persons from outside the household and, possibly, from the neighborhood are usually in attendance. A young wife who resided in the household of her father-in-law had suffered for several days from a painful toothache. Older members of the household decided that it might be the result of a curse from her recently deceased father and arranged a ceremony to remove the curse. One of the older men of the household, a shaman, conducted the ceremony; others in attendance included the patient's husband, another adult man and two adult women from the household, a neighboring adult woman, and the patient's mother and married sister from a different household and neighborhood, as well as several children who had accompanied the adults. Such ceremonies recruit those persons most intimately concerned with the patient's welfare who happen to be available at the time.

The more critical the illness, the more persons attend the curing ceremony. If the first ceremony does not remove the illness, succeeding ceremonies become more elaborate, and, as the gravity of the illness becomes apparent, more persons become concerned over the patient—particularly, if the patient is an adult. At such a ceremony, all adult members of the household are usually present, as are a majority of the neighborhood adults. Also in attendance are those close relatives of the patient (for example, siblings, siblings-in-law, parents, parents-in-law) who live in other neighborhoods. One such ceremony I attended for a critically ill man who later died was attended by all adults from his household, his aged mother and three married brothers (all from different households and neighborhoods), and several adults from each of the neighboring households.

Certain of the thanksgiving *(selamat)* ceremonies rely more heavily upon exclusive neighborhood participation. The range of invitations depends largely upon the reasons for the ceremony. While I was in Sitangkai, a group of men heard that an approaching tidal wave threatened to wipe out the village. When the wave failed to arrive, a selamat ceremony was held in the mosque by the entire Muslim Bajau community, since Allah had saved all from the disaster. On another occasion, the roof of a house was torn off by a freak wind that passed through a section of Sitangkai. No one was injured in the household, so a selamat was held, to which the neighborhood and other kinsmen of the household were invited. These people were those most grateful for the safety of the members of the household; nonrelatives in other parts of Sitangkai were less concerned and consequently did not attend.

Persons most intimately involved in the marriage of an individual are, of course, members of his household. Once the brideprice has been agreed upon, members of the household of the groom-to-be (never his parents) set about to collect the money. His parents provide the largest contribution, while the remaining amount is collected equally from their siblings, unless some are unusually poor or unusually wealthy, in which cases they may be expected to contribute less or more than others. Siblings split by personal quarrels rarely contribute to the brideprice of one another's children. Should the groom's parents have no or few siblings, first cousins or uncles and aunts may be asked to contribute. Rarely, however, is the collection extended to this degree. Each contribution is noted by the groom's parents, so that equal amounts may be returned when the contributors must raise a brideprice for their own sons.

Distribution of the brideprice among the bride's family follows similar lines. After wedding expenses are deducted, the money is distributed among the bride's parents' siblings, according to what they have contributed to past ceremonies sponsored by the bride's parents. What is left is kept by the bride's parents.

Preparations for the actual wedding celebration are mostly in the household where it will be held, although some siblings of the parents of both the bride and groom usually assist. Also, neighbors of the sponsoring household usually help decorate the house, cook food, or play music. Attendance at the evening celebration which precedes the ceremony and at the actual ceremony always includes a much wider group of kinsmen, nonkinsmen, and even some non-Bajau. Incision ceremonies and some of the more elaborate healing ceremonies follow the same pattern. If money is needed, it is collected from the most immediate kinsmen, who also assist in the planning and organization. The actual ceremony is attended by less closely related or even unrelated persons, and sometimes even non-Bajau.

At death, too, members of a household call upon other kinsmen to mourn their loss. Usually a person, or persons, within the household supervises the funeral activities, but in a small household, where all members are sorely grieved at the death, outside persons must sometimes take over making the arrangements. Household members, other immediate kinsmen, and neighbors are most intimately involved in the funeral, but all relatives and sometimes nonkinsmen drop by the house to pay their final respects to the deceased. Mourners leave money at the household to help defray the funeral expenses; and the household keeps a record of the money, in the event of a death in the donating household. Again, the pattern is the same: organization and preparations are in the hands of nuclear kinsmen, whereas other participation extends to less closely related persons and even to nonkinsmen. Anyone may attend the ceremonies before and after burial, but, in the event of succeeding ceremonies, the household extends invitations only to certain persons.

In some ways the work teams at Sitangkai are simply a solidification of the fluid, ephemeral alliances characteristic of the boat-dwelling Bajau of Tawi-Tawi. Differences, however, distinguish the Tawi-Tawi and Sitangkai societies.

The boat-dwellers' work teams more typically consist of members of a single nuclear family than do those of the house-dwellers. This is partly due to the more migratory nature of the boat-dwellers' lives, which, in turn, is related to ecological factors. Fishing grounds are more dispersed in Tawi-Tawi, and to fully exploit the monthly fishing cycles it is necessary for a family to cover a large area of sea. On the other hand, Sitangkai is surrounded by a huge reef which can be fished at all times of the month without traveling great distances from the village. As a result, a Sitangkai fisherman is usually away from his house for no longer than a day or two at a stretch, and he consequently leaves his wife and children at home. But to most profitably exploit the Tawi-Tawi fishing grounds, a Bajau must sometimes be a week or two, or even longer, away from his home moorage. And, since his fishing boat is also his home, his wife and children travel with him— sometimes with other houseboats, but frequently alone. And even if the Tawi-Tawi Bajau lived in a house his wife and children most likely would accompany him on extended fishing trips; at any rate, this is what happens among the Sitangkai Bajau, who always take wives and children with them if they expect to be away from the village for any length of time. If the boat-dwellers fish the nearby moorage waters, they usually do so alone or with another male companion or two in a small boat, while wives and children remain at home. This pattern has persisted among the Sitangkai Bajau, who not only can conveniently fish nearby waters daily without their families but also have full access to fishing boats for such trips, since they no longer serve as the family dwellings. Thus, perhaps, ecology, which demands a more migratory life in Tawi-Tawi than in Sitangkai, is more important in determining the structure of Bajau fishing work teams than is the house-dwelling habit, per se.

Another distinctive feature of the Sitangkai male work teams is their uxorilocal bias, a bias not found among the boat-dwellers. This is, of course, determined by the uxorilocal residence practiced in Sitangkai which, as noted several times previously, has been partially determined by the boat-dwellers' ideal of residence.

Sitangkai female work teams are even more exclusively uxorilocal and more permanent than is the case among the Tawi-Tawi Bajau females. This is, of course, due to the uxorilocal and sedentary nature of the Sitangkai households.

Expecting this uxorilocal bias, the alliances of the two groups are not greatly different structurally; they tend to be based on sibling-sibling, or child-parent relationships, or their affinal counterparts. The Sitangkai align for a greater variety of tasks than do their Tawi-Tawi kinsmen, who are, for the most part, fishermen. But, when aligning for these other tasks, such as stevedoring or box-making, the familiar structure of the boat-dwellers' alliances prevails.

The fact that ceremonial work teams at Sitangkai consist almost exclusively of men is definitely an indication of Islamic influence. However, even among the boat-dwellers, ceremonies are usually led by males who are familiar with bits of Islamic ritual, with an occasional important female shaman who also participates actively. Given this bias toward male leadership and Islamic ritual, it is not surprising to discover that, when more fully exposed to the Islam of the land-dwellers, the Bajau elaborated this traditional theme, since it was already in keeping with acceptable Islamic patterns.

NOTES

1. It may be necessary to note here that smuggling does not have the illicit or illegal connotations in Sulu that it has in other parts of the Philippines. In Sulu, it is simply a continuation of age-old trade relations between the archipelago and Borneo. The national boundary which separates Sulu and Borneo has tended to make this trade more difficult and considerably more profitable, but has not detracted from the prestige of the profession. Thus the status of smugglers in Sulu is comparable to that of successful businessmen elsewhere.

10. The Localized Kindred

Although it is impossible to draw bold lines around any one kindred in Sitang-kai, those of the house-dwellers in Sitangkai are easier to discern than those of the Tawi-Tawi Bajau. This is due mostly to the more sedentary life of the Sitangkai people. Upon marriage, a young couple chooses the parental household where they will probably remain most of their lives, the household of the wife. The child born of the marriage will have two large groups of kinsmen—his father's and his mother's generalized kindreds. However, because of the nature of his parents' residence, he will usually be more intimately involved in the affairs of his mother's localized kindred than those of his father's. When the boy reaches adulthood, if he marries a girl who is not a member of his mother's localized kindred he will probably reside in her household, which is likely to be in a different part of the village. On the other hand, most of the female children will remain in their mother's localized kindred upon marriage. The members of one's generalized kindred are scattered throughout Sitangkai, but the practice of ux-orilocal residence has localized solid cores of closely related persons in three residential areas of the village, and it is one of these three localized kindreds that a Bajau identifies as his kin group. Keep in mind, however, that just as many, and possibly more, members of his generalized kindred may be scattered throughout the other two localized kindreds, as well as the other Bajau villages in Sibutu, Tawi-Tawi, and Semporna.

Geographically the three localized kindreds are fairly distinct from one another, although households at the borders sometimes hold allegiances to two groups. Connected by boardwalks to the heart of town, one localized kindred is located south of the main canal that runs east-west, while the other two are located on the northern side of the canal, one almost completely connected by boardwalks to the main part of town, and the other at sea, unconnected, to the main part of town. The two localized kindreds connected to the town by board-walks are—perhaps not surprisingly—those most acculturated to Islam and furnish the majority of the mosque congregation. The most seaward one is the least acculturated, and only a few of its younger members regularly attend the mosque services. The less acculturated, localized kindred, originally from Omapoi, was the last to arrive at Sitangkai, apparently only about ten years ago, and is the only one with some full-time boat-dwellers.

A fourth localized kindred is emerging which possibly will be recognizable as distinct from the others within a few years. The acculturated localized kindred north of the canal originally came from Tandowak; the first arrivals came shortly before World War II, while other members are still arriving. The later arrivals are less acculturated to Islam and the urban life of Sitangkai and consequently have built their houses some distance seaward of the early immigrants. Members of this less acculturated segment feel uncomfortable around their more sophisticated kinsmen, who generally view them as country cousins. These differing degrees of acculturation have tended to split the group, and, although they still identify as members of a single, localized kindred, their work and ceremonial alliances indicate a cleavage. Either the less acculturated group will identify more closely with the other half as they become more acculturated to Islam, or the separation will continue, and a fourth localized kindred will emerge.

Structurally, each localized kindred can be divided into single nuclear families, of which the husband acts as head; several nuclear families dwell together, usually uxorilocally, in one house, with one of the men being recognized as the household head; in turn, each household is a member of a neighborhood consisting of four to eight houses connected by various kin ties (usually uxorilineal) and headed by one of the older men; particular neighborhoods interact through the various kin-based work and ceremonial alliances and together form localized kindreds, each of which has a headman. The three localized kindreds form the Bajau community of Sitangkai.

In addition to geography and structure, certain social activities identify the individual localized kindreds. Each has a headman who lives in the largest house with the largest household within the group. He handles any serious disputes and sometimes solemnizes weddings, and his home serves as the central gathering place for the localized kindred. The maggambit fish drives are organized by and are predominantly composed of a single localized kindred. Anyone in the community is welcome to join the drive, but its leaders, as well as most of its members, come from one localized kindred. Every third lunar month at full moon, the shamans of each kindred dance at the household of the headman, in order to capture the supernatural power believed to be flowing through the universe at such times. Each localized kindred holds its dances at its headman's house on one of three succeeding nights. Shamans of the three different localized kindreds dance at each other's dances, but the majority of each dancing group is from the sponsoring localized kindred. Persons also reveal their localized-kindred affiliations at the annual maggomboh, or first-fruits ceremony, held after the dry-rice harvest. A main ceremony is held at the house of the headman and is attended by most of the heads of the other localized-kindred households. Following this, smaller ceremonies are held in other households. Many members who have married into other localized kindreds return to attend their natal localized kindred's ceremonies, but, for the most part, attendance is drawn from the residential area. Another feature of the maggomboh celebration, the *magkanduli,* a religious ceremony held on Siculan Island, also reveals localized-kindred affiliation. The shamans of the localized kindreds and most other adult members travel to the

Members of a localized kindred pull in the catch after one of the large maggambit fish drives in the Sitangkai waters.

island to honor ancestral spirits at the special ceremony. Each localized kindred goes to the island on a different day.

The two features, perhaps, which seem to distinguish the Sitangkai localized kindred from its boat-dwelling counterpart in Tawi-Tawi most sharply, are its uxorilocal bias and its larger size. Like many apparently new features in Sitangkai social organization, however, these are innate to the boat-dwelling society.

Concerning the uxorilocality characteristic of the Sitangkai Bajau community, little need be added at this point to preceding discussions. Suffice it to repeat that the uxorilocality displayed at Sitangkai is the fulfillment of an only partly realizable pattern of residence desired by the Tawi-Tawi boat-dwellers. The larger size of the Sitangkai kindred is primarily due to the great concentration of Bajau in that community. As noted, ecological factors allow for a greater concentration of population in Sitangkai than in Tawi-Tawi. Because of the dispersed nature of the Bajau community of Tawi-Tawi, members of a single generalized kindred are scattered over a wider area than they would be in Sitangkai. As a result, any one family usually identifies with at least two, and sometimes three, localized kindreds in as many different boat villages. In many respects these several localized kindreds are subdivisions of what has become a single, large localized kindred in Sitangkai. If the Tawi-Tawi Bajau were all attracted to a single village, as has happened at Sitangkai, many of the presently identifiable localized kindreds would merge to form larger localized kindreds. At present, the boat-dwelling localized kindreds recognize close kin affinities with localized kindreds of other moorages, which the movements of individual members verify. It is, of course, the nomadic, boat-dwelling habit that keeps the branches of the localized kindred separated. Eliminate the need to wander a sea area, eliminate the boat-dwelling life, and provide an attraction to a central area, and the Tawi-Tawi boat-dwellers would replicate the Sitangkai pattern, in which, as peripheral kindred members moved to Sitangkai from other Bajau villages, they tended to become incorporated into an existing localized kindred rather than to form their own.

The Sitangkai headman has jurisdiction not unlike that of his boat-dwelling counterpart, except that he tends to be more specialized as an arbitrator. This greater specialization seems related to the greater size of the Sitangkai localized kindred and the general trend toward occupational specialization among the Sitangkai Bajau. The boat-dwelling headman always has duties beyond his judicial role as headman; he frequently solemnizes weddings, acts as shaman, and officiates at incision ceremonies, and he sometimes leads fishing groups. However, in Sitangkai, he serves almost full-time as an arbitrator and leaves other duties to other specialists, primarily because the larger population generates more disputes which he must settle. And, since his chief function, even among the boat-dwellers, is that of arbitration, it may be expected that, as the need for arbitration increases, his role in other activities decreases. This has happened at Sitangkai.

Most household quarrels in Sitangkai are handled by the members themselves, though sometimes neighbors may be called in to arbitrate. Should the members be unable to reach agreement, or if the matter is serious or extends beyond the household or neighborhood, it is taken to the headman. The disputants present their sides to the headman, who, after discussion with all present, gives his decision. When the case is especially difficult, the headman calls in several older men of the localized kindred to hear the case and offer advice. If a fine is levied, one half goes to the offended person and the other half to the headman.

Ideally, the headmanship passes from father to eldest son, but, like most ideals, this does not always reflect reality. In fact, only one of the three major headmen in Sitangkai inherited his position this way. In one case the position went to the youngest of seven brothers, partly because the older brothers were not interested in the position or had married outside the residential area of the localized kindred, and partly because the youngest had attended school and was exceptionally bright. In the other case, the old headman had only one son who, although he lived in the residential area of the localized kindred, was not at all qualified for the position. Consequently, the position passed on to the eldest son-in-law of the headman, who was only distantly related to the old man, but had outstanding leadership qualities.

Although there is much interaction among the localized kindreds, nonetheless each could be fairly self-sufficient. Each has a headman to arbitrate serious disputes among its members. Each has shamans to take care of illnesses of a supernatural nature and herbalists to attend to physical illnesses. Excepting the unacculturated localized kindred, each has an imam to handle Islamic ritual. Boat-builders are contracted within the localized kindred for new boats and boat repairs. Members of work and ceremonial alliances are generally drawn from the localized kindred, and marriage-partners may be taken from the same group.

In no sense, however, are localized kindreds closed social units. Marriages between the localized kindreds tend to unite them; the shaman cult has members from all localized kindreds; the fish drives, although sponsored by localized kindreds, always have some outside participants; large ceremonies like weddings and incisions always have outside guests; the major Islamic celebrations in the mosque always cross localized-kindred lines; and the public school classes, of course, indiscriminately mix the children of the several localized kindreds.

11. The Village

The three Bajau localized kindreds comprise two-thirds of Sitangkai's population. And, although each Bajau's activities normally involve only his kindred, there are occasions when nonkin, or village associations, emerge. In this respect also, he differs from the Tawi-Tawi Bajau, who rarely—almost never—aligns with nonkinsmen.

More than anything else in Sitangkai, the mosque most effectively crosses kin lines. Although the original mosque was built by one localized kindred, the present mosque was constructed with donations from all three localized kindreds, especially the two most acculturated ones. Persons from all three localized kindreds regularly attend the Friday services and other Muslim celebrations, and all three localized kindreds are represented on the board of directors. Any mosque repairs are made by work groups which disregard kindred affiliation.

The leading members of the mosque are regularly invited to attend and perform Islamic ceremonies, even if they are not members of the sponsoring localized kindred. The less acculturated localized kindred, especially, depends upon the more learned men of the mosque to officiate at its Islamic ceremonies, which its members have only recently begun to observe and learn. Although few members of this less acculturated localized kindred take active part in the mosque services, many, especially the younger men, regularly attend, sitting on the sides to observe the ritual. It seems only a matter of a few years before this localized kindred will be as acculturated to Islam as the other two.

It should be remembered, however, that participation in Islamic ritual is limited almost exclusively to males. A few females with fine chanting voices are sometimes invited to participate in ceremonies, but, for the most part, the ceremonies are male affairs. Women's participation is usually limited to preparing refreshments, and most often the women at a single event are from one neighborhood or are closely related to one another, if from different neighborhoods, and are kinsmen. Only at community services held in the mosque do unrelated women prepare refreshments together. Such unrelated women, of course, pray together during the mosque services, but they usually attend the mosque in small kin groups, pray in these groups, and leave together with little interaction with other women. Such is not the case with the men, who range further in the social field and have many nonkinsmen friends whom they have met in fishing or at the wharf while stevedoring.

The shaman cult also effectively cuts localized kindred lines. Although each localized kindred has its own shamans, who take care of its supernatural matters, the shamans themselves, especially the men, identify closely with one another because of their common interests and the dances they perform together every four months. The shamans occasionally confer on particularly grave matters. While I was in Sitangkai, a rash of personal quarrels broke out between members of the different localized kindreds. Rumors spread that evil spirits were causing the quarrels, so the leading shamans of the three localized kindreds met to conduct a ceremony to rid the village of them. The spirit boat described for the Tawi-Tawi Bajau is also constructed by the Sitangkai shamans for the same purpose—to rid the village of evil spirits. The leading shamans of all three localized kindreds organize the construction of the boat. Upon completion, they pull it throughout the village waters as they dance and chant to attract the disease-causing spirits. It is then taken to the open sea and set adrift, in hopes that the disease-causing spirits are aboard and will drift away from the village.

This unifying aspect of religion, both Islam and shamanism, is not unique to the house-dwelling Bajau. As noted, of the only two activities which effectively cross kin-lines to unify the boat-dwelling villagers, one is the religious ceremony held periodically to rid the community of evil spirits. In addition, funeral ceremonies and certain healing ceremonies among the boat-dwellers are often composed of nonkinsmen. Religion, then, is important for community organization in both groups. It reaches its greatest manifestation at Sitangkai because of the more formal organization of religion, both Islam and the shaman cult, there and because of the more scheduled and frequent performance of religious ritual, as in the weekly mosque services and the annual cycle of Islamic ceremonies. Both Islam and shamanism at Sitangkai are, however, aspects of the boat-dwelling culture which have been formalized and expanded.

Although the guests for Sitangkai wedding and incision celebrations are drawn largely from the sponsoring localized kindred, Bajau from other kindred and even non-Bajau are always present. Also, as noted earlier, the fish drives attract persons from other localized kindreds, even though they are sponsored by one localized kindred and most of the fishermen come from that group.

The public schools have also been effective in breaking through kinship walls. At school, children frequently develop close friendships with nonkinsmen that extend into adulthood. And, since social stratification among the Bajau is partly determined by education, and education and Islam tend to go hand-in-hand, a Bajau may identify more closely with an educated, Muslim nonkinsman than with an uneducated, non-Muslim kinsman.

The school cliques also have their parallel among the boat-dwellers. Although because of the nomadic life of the Tawi-Tawi Bajau most children's play groups are composed of siblings or first cousins, children of the more sedentary families who remain in one village for long periods of time often develop friendships with nonkinsmen who are also sedentary members of the village. I do not have the time-depth to estimate the duration or strength of these friendships, but, judging from adult patterns of friendship and association, they do not extend too strongly into adulthood, as many do in Sitangkai. Nonetheless, the basis for such nonkin associations is found among the boat-dwellers; at Sitangkai they have been elaborated through a thoroughly sedentary life and the public school system.

Bajau political structure also tends to unite the three localized kindred. Although each localized kindred has its own headman, when problems cross localized-kindred lines, other political machinery begins to operate. A historical sketch will explain the evolution of the system:

The old headman, Alari, who built the first Bajau house in Sitangkai was one of the strongest leaders ever known among the Bajau. Although his localized kindred originally came from Tanduwak and is not considered the "first family" of Sitangkai, his own strong personality elevated him to leadership over all the Sitangkai Bajau. American administrators early recognized this, and all their dealings with the Bajau were via Alari. During Alari's time, each headman handled the disputes of his own localized kindred, except that when these disputes crossed localized-kindred lines, Alari was called in to arbitrate. Thus, he came to be recognized by both the American administrators and the Bajau as the headman of Sitangkai. Upon his death, his position of leadership passed to his youngest son, Ingguan, who, in addition to having inherited his father's strong personality, was also one of the few Bajau at that time who had attended school. As with Alari, it was through Ingguan that the rest of Sitangkai's officials communicated to the Bajau community. However, this informal arrangement had to be formalized during the late 1950s, when Sulu Province elected its first political officers; before that time, officers had been appointed by representatives of the national government in Jolo. The existing village political structure of the rest of the Philippines was, of course, the model after which Sulu was patterned—an elected village council led by a headman. The first such administrative body in Sitangkai was appointed in the late forties, and the first elected group took office in 1959. Whoever appointed the first council wisely appointed Ingguan as one member; the other four and the headman were non-Bajau. The same men were elected to office in the first elections, and, as a result, the traditional Bajau political system has been little altered by the new system. Headmen still handle problems within their own localized kindreds; if the problems are too grave or if they cross localized-kindred lines, they are taken to Ingguan; if they are too grave for Ingguan to handle, or if they involve non-Bajau, they are taken to the village council. If the village council cannot reach an agreement or needs higher authority, the mayor of Sitangkai is consulted.

Within Sitangkai, the mayor is the strongest political figure. Theoretically, the village council governs Sitangkai, and they, like other village councils in Sibutu, are accountable to the mayor, who governs the Sibutu Islands District. However, in reality, the mayor heads the Sitangkai village council and rules Sitangkai with no weak hand. To the Bajau he is the final word and the court of last appeal. And because in many respects he is a continuation of the datu system that operated under the sultanate, his autocratic tactics are in keeping with traditional patterns.

Two important features distinguish the Sitangkai Bajau political structure from that of the boat-dwellers: the greater authority of the leaders and a more formal structure. As noted, the headman among the boat-dwellers acts primarily as an adviser or consultant; he hears the case (if the case is even taken to him), offers a verdict (which may or may not be accepted), and levies a fine (which probably is never paid). His lack of power seems due primarily to the nomadic life of these Bajau. The boat-dwellers normally divide their allegiance between two villages (that of the husband and that of the wife), and should the headman of one of these villages prove too demanding, the couple can easily move on to another village and a less demanding headman. Consequently, the headman exerts little authority. Such is not the case, however, among the house-dwelling Bajau. These Bajau cannot so easily pick up and leave, so they must follow the decision of the headman—a decision which usually has the consensus of the group—or suffer the social ostracism their disobedience might otherwise bring. Because of the larger size of the Sitangkai localized kindreds and the greater numbers of individuals under one headman, the Sitangkai headman more commonly calls in other older men to assist in decision-making than does the Tawi-Tawi headman. This is especially true in cases involving persons whom the headman does not know intimately. As a result, the headman's decision gains even more weight by the backing of a group of respected elders. And since the Sitangkai headmen are recognized by the mayor of Sitangkai as the leaders of their localized kindreds, they can always call in his authority to support their decisions. The decision of the leading headman of Sitangkai, the one who holds a seat on the village council, is almost always respected, since he not only represents the highest authority in the Bajau community, but also has the support of the village council, the mayor, and, ultimately, the governor of Sulu. Because of these two factors—the sedentary way of life and the power structure of the political system—the house-dwelling Bajau tend to heed the decisions of their headman more often than do their Tawi-Tawi kinsmen.

The boat-dwelling political structure is much more amorphous, although it contains hazy outlines of the formal structure that has emerged at Sitangkai. Each localized kindred has a headman. Each boat village with more than one localized kindred recognizes one of its headmen as head of the entire village, when such recognition is necessary. Traditionally, the boat-dwellers held some sort of unclear allegiance to local datus, who, in turn, owed allegiance to the Sultan of Sulu. However, in reality, the Bajau were beyond the pale of the sultanate's concerns and were allowed to follow their sea-borne lives with little interference. This same pattern has continued in Tawi-Tawi through the present political system. Nonetheless, Sitangkai's political system has its outlines in the traditional structure of the boat-dwelling society and is in no sense original.

Social stratification is more pronounced among the Sitangkai Bajau than among the Tawi-Tawi Bajau. Class lines are determined by wealth and acculturation to Islam; frequently the two go hand in hand, but not always. The five Bajau hadji and their families form the elite of Sitangkai Bajau society. They, or their immediate ancestors, were the first Bajau to build houses and to embrace Islam. Few of them are fishermen, and most were at one time involved in smuggling, from which they accumulated considerable wealth. Many of them have attended school, and all their children presently attend. Below them are the other Muslim Bajau who regularly attend the mosque services; some of these are still fishermen, but many are stevedores or are in other nonfishing jobs. Most children of this group also attend school, but fewer of their parents have attended. The next group consists of the large number of families who only occasionally or never attend the mosque; most of these are fishermen who live at the periphery of the physical, as well as the Islamic, community. At the very bottom of Sitangkai society are those few fishing families who still dwell in boats. They never attend the mosque, never send their children to school, and are considered pagans by the acculturated Bajau as well as by the non-Bajau of Sitangkai. Only about ten such families, however, still live in boats, and probably within a year or two they will have abandoned the boat-dwelling habit and thereby will have climbed a rung up the social ladder.

Bajau relations with the non-Bajau people of Sitangkai are, for the most part, smooth and friendly, especially compared to some other parts of Sulu, where the Bajau are considered untouchables by their neighbors. This seems to be partly because the Bajau comprise the majority of the Sitangkai population and partly because the Sitangkai Bajau are more acculturated to Islam than any other Bajau group in Sulu. As noted, the majority of non-Bajau live in the houses and shops along the main canal, or immediately adjacent, and in the houses that still fringe Sitangkai Island. A few other non-Bajau houses, especially those of fish-buyers, are scattered among the Bajau houses at sea.

As a group, the Bajau still suffer social discrimination because of their former, and in some cases, present, pagan religious beliefs. Even though some Bajau are more devout Muslims than many land-dwellers, their mosque is sometimes referred to by the land-dwellers as the mosque of the pagans. Nonetheless, the most acculturated Bajau elite are regularly invited to attend ceremonies of the land-dwellers and a few have married into land-dwelling families. One Bajau woman is married to a Chinese, an unheard-of situation in other parts of Sulu, and another is one of the five wives of the mayor—an obviously political marriage.

Intervillage kin ties are fewer and less important among the Sibutu than among the Tawi-Tawi Bajau. Part of this is because Sitangkai has such a large concentration of Bajau and, if one is from there, virtually all his significant kinsmen live in Sitangkai. If the present trend of migration to Sitangkai from the outer villages continues, the Bajau villages at Omapoi and Tanduwak will probably disappear within the next decade. Tungnehat is still a sizable Bajau community and most likely will remain so unless unforeseeable events cause a movement to Sitangkai. With the abandonment of boat-dwelling, related persons have become localized in single villages and their kin ties to other villages have become less significant. Intervillage marriage is still fairly common, however, and the villages retain kin ties through the maggomboh ceremony. Nonetheless, one cannot discuss all the

Bajau villages in Sibutu as a single community, as he may all the Tawi-Tawi Bajau moorages. Each Sibutu Bajau village views itself as unique. Such cannot be said for the Tawi-Tawi moorages.

Many Sitangkai Bajau have kinsmen in Tawi-Tawi, but they normally are not close kinsmen, except for those few families who have recently married Tawi-Tawi people. The greater acculturation to Islam of the Sitangkai people has been effective in bringing about a cleavage between themselves and the Tawi-Tawi people. Should the Tawi-Tawi people accept Islam, as they doubtless will within the next couple of decades or so, their ties to Sitangkai may become closer. As it is, they are still considered a pagan, almost untouchable, group by the Tawi-Tawi land-dwellers, and the Sitangkai Bajau are none too eager to claim them as kinsmen.

On the other hand, the Sitangkai people closely identify with the small Bajau village of Bangau-Bangau on the outskirts of Semporna, Sabah. Many of the Bangau-Bangau Bajau have only recently moved to Sabah from Sitangkai and still regularly visit their Sitangkai kinsmen. They, like the Sitangkai people, are acculturated to Islam and are, in general, regarded as sophisticated urbanites by their Sitangkai relatives.

Part Three

SUMMARY AND CONCLUSIONS

12. Processes of Change

This study compares and contrasts two groups of Bajau of the Sulu Islands, namely the boat-dwellers of Tawi-Tawi and the house-dwellers of Sitangkai, in order to discover what changes have occurred in Bajau society as a result of the abandonment of the nomadic boat-life and the acceptance of a house-dwelling way of life. The recurring theme has been that the seemingly new patterns of social behavior found among the house-dwelling Sitangkai Bajau are actually not new to Bajau society, but are found, albeit less elaborated, in the traditional boat-dwelling society. This position makes the fairly obvious assumption that every society has certain forms of behavior that it regards as preferable and that may actually dominate in practice, which are based on the jural rules of the society. As noted, this feature of society has conventionally been called social structure. But every society also reveals behavioral patterns which deviate from these preferred forms but which are tolerated as legitimate practices when the ideals cannot be practiced. The possibility of choosing among alternative patterns of behavior, or what Firth calls social organization, is the genesis of change in the dominant behavior patterns and ultimately, possibly, in the structure. When members of a society find themselves in a new position where the preferred forms cannot be followed, they turn to those sanctioned alternatives which are most congruent to the new social milieu. And since the new social milieu is often the result of contact with a superordinate, imposing society, those patterns of traditional behavior which most closely approximate the models of the imposing group will be those chosen by the changing society. Only if the traditionally preferred patterns and all the traditionally sanctioned patterns can no longer be practiced does the society look elsewhere to perhaps borrow from other societies. I contend, however, that borrowing of this sort is not common.

This view of society—that is, that it has dominant as well as alternative patterns of behavior—is preferable to more traditional notions, which assume that only one pattern of behavior can arise from a given social structure, since this view can better illustrate the ways in which structural change occurs. The majority of anthropological studies purporting to deal with social change give little understanding of the processes of change, but, rather, tell only that one social form became another social form, with little explanation of why the change followed the particular patterns it did (Barth 1967). Most commonly, acculturation is said to have occurred—that is, the changing social forms are due to the influence of an intruding society, and the new forms may have, in fact, been borrowed from the new society. Even if this may be the case, such studies fail to account for the operating processes underlying the changing behavioral patterns. Firth's concepts of structure and of organization, and the presence of what I have called preferred and alternative patterns of social behavior, overcome this omission. Not only do the concepts more realistically reveal patterns of social behavior as flexible and dynamic, but they also offer an explanation of why social change follows the patterns that it does.

My comparative analysis of the traditional boat-dwelling Bajau society and the house-dwelling Bajau society has demonstrated the validity of this position, as will be illustrated by a review of eleven aspects of Bajau society—household composition, household residence, village residence, marriage, divorce, kinship terminology, the neighborhood, action groups, the kindred, political structure, and religion:

1. HOUSEHOLD COMPOSITION. The boat-dwelling Bajau household is typically a single nuclear family, whereas that of the house-dwelling Bajau is more typically an extended uxorilocal household. Some few boat-dwellers live in extended-family households if the houseboat is large enough or if a newly married couple has not yet acquired its own houseboat, but the size of the houseboat generally limits the size of the household to a single nuclear family. It is, nonetheless, a commonly voiced ideal among the boat-dwellers that it is best to live intimately with one's kinsmen—ideally one's uxorilateral kinsmen—even though these ideals, for the most part, cannot be practiced. Given these ideals, it would seem likely that if the boat-people had larger dwellings and if circumstances altered so that they could practice uxorilocal residence, they would live in uxorilocal extended-family households. Such is precisely what has happened at Sitangkai. This form of extended family is not a case of acculturation to the Islamic neighbors, for they, in contrast to the Bajau, tend to live in single, nuclear-family households.

2. UXORILOCAL RESIDENCE. Among the house-dwelling Bajau, the patterns of residence of individual couples also tend to reflect a preference of uxorilocality. As my data have revealed, this preference has its genesis in the boat-dwelling society, as an ideal where it cannot be practiced; in Sitangkai, however, the ideal pattern has been realized. Because the Muslim land-dwellers more commonly reside virilocally, uxorilocal residence among the Bajau cannot be considered acculturation, but is more empirically demonstrated as the realization of a preexisting Bajau ideal.

3. NATOLOCAL VILLAGE RESIDENCE. The greater percentage of natolocal village residence at Sitangkai is in great contrast to the varied moorage residence found among the boat-dwellers. The Sitangkai pattern is primarily the result of having the large concentration of Bajau in a single village. Such a concentration allows the house-dwelling youth to find a marriage-partner easily in his home village, whereas the smaller populations of the moorages of the boat-dwellers make it less easy for a youth to find a bride in his home moorage, much as he would prefer it, and he consequently must commonly marry outside. Although

the land-dwelling Muslims more often reside in their natolocal villages than do the boat-dwelling Bajau, the high percentage of such residence among the Sitang-kai Bajau cannot be convincingly explained as acculturation to the Muslims. It is more understandable as the result of the larger village size which enables more of these Bajau to follow a preferred pattern.

4. FIRST-COUSIN MARRIAGE. The boat-dwelling Bajau are free to marry any first cousins except patrilateral parallel cousins or those with whom they have been reared intimately. Among the Sitangkai house-dwelling Bajau, a general disapproval of all first-cousin marriage is emerging. The Sitangkai pattern is mostly an intensification of the traditional patterns. Since most Sitangkai Bajau live in uxorilocal households, first cousins of the household are raised together intimately and are thereby improper marriage-partners by traditional mores. In addition, the traditional prohibition against marriage of patrilateral parallel cous-ins has been retained at Sitangkai. As a result, a good share of one's first cousins are improper marriage-partners—more so than among the boat-dwellers, because of their smaller households and nomadic movements. The strong disapproval of all first cousin marriage by land-dwelling Muslims has, no doubt, also been a factor in the Sitangkai extension of the prohibition to all first cousins. Nonethe-less, acculturation alone does not explain the emergence of the prohibition. The Muslims presented to the Sitangkai Bajau a model partly in keeping with their traditional preferences, with the result that they reworked their traditional pat-terns of cousin-marriage to more closely approximate the Muslim model.

5. DIVORCE. The house-dwelling Bajau have a much higher divorce-rate than do the boat-dwelling Bajau. However, the sentiments which lead to divorce among the house-dwellers can be found in the boat-dwelling society—namely, that one's loyalty belongs first and primarily to kinsmen. This loyalty is more often threatened by house-dwelling than by boat-dwelling. The house-dwelling Bajau groom usually goes to live in his bride's extended uxorilocal household; he frequently does not know his bride or her kinsmen well and is consequently a stranger in the household. Thus, when conflicts arise between him and his bride or between him and his bride's kinsmen, the household unites against him, and he commonly leaves in frustration to seek a divorce. On the other hand, the boat-dwelling couple lives alone in its own boat and does not have a large group of kinsmen to meddle in the early marital quarrels. Partly because of this, their marriages tend to be more stable than those of the house-dwellers. Nonetheless, in both societies one's loyalties are expected to remain with one's kinsmen, and such is usually the case in the early days of marriage before loyalties have been transferred to spouses. But because of the differences in household composition and kin relationships, loyalties conflict differently in the two societies. The in-crease in divorce at Sitangkai cannot be explained as an acculturation to Muslim society because the Muslims divorce even less than the boat-dwelling Bajau and often criticize the frequent divorce of the Sitangkai Bajau.

6. KINSHIP TERMINOLOGY. Kinship terminology among the house-dwellers tends to be more classificatory than that of the boat-dwellers. Only on rare

occasions do the boat-dwellers extend kin terms of the nuclear family to more distantly related kinsmen or even to nonkinsmen, to indicate intimate relationships. Among the house-dwellers, on the other hand, nuclear-family kin terms are commonly extended collaterally to household mates. The principle involved is that both groups extend nuclear-family terms to reflect intimacy, and, since among the house-dwellers several nuclear families live intimately in a single household, it should come as no surprise that they more commonly extend the terms beyond the nuclear family. This extension of kin terms by the house-dwellers has not been borrowed from the Muslims, who employ a descriptive kinship terminology and who, in fact, often express astonishment at the casual manner in which the Bajau extend nuclear-family terms.

7. THE NEIGHBORHOOD. The kin-based neighborhood is much more important as a social group among the house-dwellers than among the boat-dwellers. Nonetheless, shades of the concept of the neighborhood are found among the boat-dwellers. In their society, the most important social unit above the nuclear family is the family-alliance unit; they have no important social group between this unit and the localized kindred. However, within the moorages, the family alliances tend to moor their houseboats near other family alliances whom they recognize as kinsmen. Essentially, the same pattern was followed when the Sitangkai Bajau moved to houses; in general, the family alliances moved to a single house which was built near other, related households to form an uxorilocal, kin-based neighborhood. Because of the sedentary life of the Sitangkai Bajau the neighborhood has become a permanent social group—unlike the boat-dwelling counterpart of a few boats moored near each other, which is extremely ephemeral. As a result, the Sitangkai neighborhood units cannot be considered the result of acculturation to land-dwelling Muslim practices; in fact, because many of the Muslim families have only recently arrived in Sitangkai as immigrants, they do not have many kinsmen near whom they could dwell, even if they wanted to do so.

8. WORK GROUPS. The Tawi-Tawi and Sitangkai Bajau reveal differences in both their work groups and their ceremonial groups. Among the boat-dwellers, the most common work group is the fishing unit, which normally consists of a man, his wife, and possibly their children. Their less common work groups for wood-working or boat-building consist of a man and his brothers or brothers-in-law. Among the house-dwellers, women less often fish with their husbands, who usually prefer brothers or brothers-in-law in their stead—as they do for other work alliances. The elimination of women from the fishing groups seems demonstrably related to three factors—ecology, house-dwelling, and acculturation. The sea environment of Tawi-Tawi demands that the boat-dwellers follow a monthly cycle that covers a fairly extensive area; consequently, it is necessary for most families who fish commercially to be away from their home villages for a couple of weeks each month. Rather than leaving his wife and family at home for such a long period (which would be almost impossible, anyway, since their home is also the fishing boat), a man usually prefers to take them with him—even though he

may have other male companions to assist him in fishing. In Sitangkai, the major fishing grounds are easily accessible to the village and so it is unnecessary to be away from the village for more than a day or so at a time. Consequently, a man is never separated from his family for long periods. Also, since the fishing boat is no longer the living quarters at Sitangkai, the wife and children may remain in the house while the husband uses the boat for fishing. An important factor that discourages the more acculturated women from fishing is the land-dwellers' notion that such work is unsuitable for them; not surprisingly, the most accul-turated women are those who fish least with their husbands. The uxorilocal bias of the male work groups reflects this same bias, which permeates much of Sitang-kai social organization. Ceremonial groups at Sitangkai are more exclusively male than are those in Tawi-Tawi. This seems due largely to the influence of Islam, in which ritual is almost exclusively in male hands. However, the Muslim model simply tends to intensify the traditional Bajau practice whereby males hold the leadership positions in ritual but permit females to participate actively. Thus, the changes in the Sitangkai work and ceremonial groups can be attributed in part to acculturation to the land-dwelling Muslim society, in the course of which the traditional Bajau dominant pattern has been reemphasized.

9. THE LOCALIZED KINDRED. Two features distinguish the house-dwelling Sitangkai localized kindreds from those found among the boat-dwelling Tawi-Tawi Bajau—their larger size and their uxorilocality. The greater size is related both to the Sitangkai abandonment of the traditional nomadic boat-life and to the ecology of the Sibutu Islands, their present habitat. As noted, the fishing reefs in Tawi-Tawi are more dispersed than are those in Sibutu, and so in order to profitably exploit the fishing grounds it is necessary for the boat-dwelling Bajau to move throughout the month. Consequently, their numbers are always scattered among several moorages throughout the area where localized kindreds congre-gate. However, in Sitangkai, because of the greater accessibility and concentration of fishing grounds and the sedentary way of life, these Bajau are able to congregate in a central area. As a result, the formerly dispersed but related localized kindreds have combined to form fewer and larger localized kindreds. The uxorilocal nature of the Sitangkai localized kindreds cannot be attributed to acculturation to the Muslim peoples, since such large uxorilocal groupings of kinsmen are not charac-teristic of the land-dwelling Muslims of Sitangkai.

10. POLITICAL STRUCTURE. The outlines of the Sitangkai political structure are evident in the traditional boat-dwelling society of Tawi-Tawi. The chief difference between the two groups is that the Sitangkai pattern has become more formal and has been incorporated into the political system of Sulu Province, which essentially follows the lines of the old sultanate. But even this is not truly unique to Sitangkai Bajau social organization, since even in traditional society the boat-dwelling Bajau owed an ill-defined allegiance to local datus, and ultimately to the sultan. In Sitangkai, Bajau have been more completely incorporated into the dominant political system, but nonetheless their present participation is simply an intensifi-cation of a less elaborated, traditional pattern.

11. ISLAM. Although I have not separately discussed religion per se, it should be fairly obvious that many of the changes which have occurred at Sitangkai are variously related to Islamic influence. But to say that the Bajau have borrowed Islam from the land-dwellers is misleading. Before Islam was introduced to Sulu, the religious beliefs and practices of both the Bajau and the non-Bajau land-dwellers were probably not significantly different. When the land-dwellers of Sulu accepted Islam, they interpreted most of it to fit existing patterns of religious belief, and their present system represents a syncretism of their traditional beliefs and those of Islam. This folk Islam then became the model which was presented to those Bajau who moved to houses in Sitangkai near the Muslim land-dwellers. Because the Bajau share the same indigenous religious beliefs as the Sulu land-dwelling Muslims and because the Bajau themselves have for many years been incorporating bits and pieces of Islam into their own religious system, it could be predicted that more intimate contact with Sulu's folk Islam would not require drastic alterations in traditional Bajau beliefs. Such has been the case among the Sitangkai house-dwelling Bajau. The Bajau there have simply intensified those aspects of their traditional system which best approximate the acceptable Muslim model of the land-dwellers. This is true also of the elaborate shaman cult at Sitangkai. Early reports (for example, Taylor) suggest that long before these Bajau moved to houses, the shaman cult was central to their religious system. Today, the Sitangkai cult is still very central and vital to Bajau culture, but it is being incorporated into Islam. For example, all shaman curing ceremonies I observed used some Islamic ritual. Some shaman ceremonies were held in the mosque, and several men served as both shamans and imams. The Bajau see no conflict in the roles, and, probably, before such conflict has arisen the shamans will have become fully amalgamated into Sulu Islam.

Changes resulting from Islamization appear to be more in the realm of values than of structure. Although I made no systematic investigation of changing values, such changes are noticeable at Sitangkai, where in comparison with the boat-dwellers the house-dwelling Bajau are more hospitable, cleaner, less shy, and have stricter premarital and extramarital sex prohibitions. These are only some of the most obvious values they have learned from their Muslim neighbors. So far these new values have not had a significant influence on social structure, but they most likely will have some effect as they are more rigidly followed.

I do not contend that all social change occurs as described in this one society, that of the Bajau, for each case is obviously somewhat different from all others. I do contend, however, that, when societies find it impossible to practice their preferred behavioral patterns, they tend first to resort to their sanctioned alternative patterns in their attempts to adapt to the new situation. Only if none of these can be practiced does a group look elsewhere for models. However, the Bajau case is somewhat unusual in two respects. First, the society with which they came into more intimate contact was not alien to them. In fact, most of Bajau history has been passed at the peripheries of the land-dwelling, non-Bajau peoples; indeed, they and the land-dwellers probably once lived as a single people (Nimmo 1968).

Such a contact situation is obviously quite different from a situation like that of the Manus Islanders of New Guinea, who lived in relative isolation until World War II, when they were suddenly invaded by thousands of American troops. Secondly, the Bajau were never forced to abandon the nomadic boat-dwelling life to become sedentary house-dwellers. Because there was little pressure on them from outside to conform to imposed behavioral patterns, they were able to continue to follow those traditional practices that proved congruent to the new, house-dwelling way of life. Obviously, the processes of change operating in such a situation are different from those which occur in societies which have been forced to adopt a particular pattern of living. Nonetheless, even if a society is invaded by a dominant alien group, or even if it is forced to adopt an alien pattern, the initial stages of the change will be characterized by those adjustments compatible with patterns existing in the traditional society.

If the house-dwelling Sitangkai Bajau society continues to follow its new patterns, some of the present alternatives (which were preferred patterns in the boat-dwelling society) may no longer be sanctioned. In other words, an actual change in structure will occur. Indications suggesting this are present in regard to residence, marriage, and religion. For example, some of the Sitangkai families still occasionally return to boat-living for fishing trips or for special ceremonies. Even such temporary boat-living is beginning to meet with disapproval from the more acculturated members of the community, who relegate such families to the lowest social positions in the Bajau community, since boat-dwelling has traditionally identified the Bajau as a pagan, outcast group—a tradition they would like to forget. Similarly, the growing Sitangkai disapproval of any kind of first-cousin marriage will probably eventually result in the norm that all first-cousin marriage is incestuous. This growing disapproval is partly due to the influence of the land-dwellers' values and partly to the earlier-mentioned structural features which make such marriages infeasible even by traditional Bajau norms. Some traditional religious beliefs which are still practiced even by some of the more Islamicized Sitangkai Bajau are also beginning to meet with disapproval and probably will eventually be condemned. Again, this is primarily due to the acceptance of the land-dwellers' notions about proper religious behavior. Thus, former preferred patterns of behavior, which are currently alternatives to new preferred patterns, will eventually be eliminated as even alternative behavioral patterns, since new values are evolving which do not condone them.

I do not intend to imply, however, that such a situation is unique to a society undergoing change as a result of culture contact. Rather, this flexible, dynamic aspect is always characteristic of societies and is responsible for bringing about and allowing change. Only when the concept of social structure is viewed as involving such a flexible, dynamic process can it be adequately used to deal with change. Otherwise, one must be content to use it to describe static, unreal societies, frozen at a moment in time.

The Bajau case has a further feature that is somewhat uncommon in the anthropological literature, in that it illustrates changes resulting from the meeting of two non-Western, "simple" societies. The bulk of anthropological literature on social change deals with the impact of advanced, Western societies on small, non-Western societies. It would seem, however, that in the long history of man the Bajau case is the more usual. Until the improvements in transportation during the past two or three centuries, it was unusual for totally alien societies to encounter one another. As the culture-area concept illustrated some years ago, individual societies do not exist as closed, unique units, but rather tend to share many cultural items with neighboring societies. Societies separated by several hundred miles may be drastically different from one another, but, because of their separation, they would rarely have occasion to interact directly. Their usual interaction would be with neighboring societies which were more like themselves. Thus, changes resulting from greater interaction between societies would not be of the dramatic sort of the past few centuries when West met non-West, but the less revolutionary sort of changes which occur when two very similar societies begin to interact more intimately than before, as the Bajau and their land-dwelling neighbors are now.

It is perhaps legitimate to ask whether the society of the Sitangkai Bajau indeed has undergone *structural* change as a result of the move from boats to houses, a question which may appear a bit delayed at the conclusion of a study claiming to deal with structural change. But the question is nonetheless relevant, and the answer largely depends on one's view of social structure. If *social structure* is defined as a model constructed from the preferred patterns of behavior within a society then, clearly, there has been a change in social structure among the Sitangkai Bajau—the composition of household and work groups, patterns of residence and marriage, and kinship terminology have all changed. On the other hand, if social structure is a model that attempts to describe the rules which apply to the total range of social behavior within a society, then one may hesitate in calling the change at Sitangkai a structural change. Essentially, the structural patterns which are found in the boat-dwelling society are still operating to pro-duce the behavioral patterns of the house-dwelling society; in fact, it is for this very reason that the alterations at Sitangkai have taken the particular direction they have. The seemingly new behavior at Sitangkai has always been sanctioned in traditional Bajau society. Thus, there have been few additions of new social behavior, but, rather, simply a reorientation of behavior. But, with the reorienta-tion, the resulting behavioral patterns among the house-dwellers have brought about a system of interpersonal relations considerably different from the system that has been operative among the boat-dwellers. Whether or not there has been a change in structure, there has been a change in behavioral patterns.

Perhaps the more important problem rests in the types of models that an-thropologists construct to describe societies, rather than in which of these models is to be called social structure. The crucial matter is that models be constructed which can be used to explore social change by revealing the dynamics of social life. It would seem that, unless such models be used for describing social struc-ture, the anthropologist will find the concept inapplicable to the dynamics of social life. Only such models reveal the variety of behavior which may serve as alternatives to the preferred patterns—that is, the varied and dynamic aspects of societies. Without revealing both these preferred and alternative patterns, the social anthropologist cannot hope to describe and understand social change.

Furthermore, it would seem that by building models which reveal the gamut of variation in social life, the anthropologist can indicate the general direction of change, once he has an understanding of the catalyst of change. If the model statistically displays both the preferred and alternative patterns of social behavior, it should be possible to indicate within a finite number of possibilities the direction which social behavior will take when its preferred patterns have been blocked or condemned. Prediction of this sort cannot be precise, but, at least such prediction is removed from the realm of complete guesswork and impression.

Bibliography

Appell, G. N. 1967. "Observational Procedures for Identifying Kindreds: Social Isolates Among the Rungus of Borneo." *Southwestern Journal of Anthropology* 23:192–207.

Barth, Fredrik. 1967. "On the Study of Social Change." *American Anthropologist* 69: 661–669.

Beals, Ralph. 1953 "Acculturation." In *Anthropology Today*. Chicago, University of Chicago Press.

Firth, Raymond. 1951. *Elements of Social Organization*. London: Watts.

Goodenough, Ward H. 1965. "Rethinking 'Status' and 'Role': Toward a General Model of the Cultural Organization of Social Relationships." In *The Relevance of Models for Social Anthropology*. ASA Monographs 1. London: Tavistock.

Keesing, Roger. 1968. "Nonunilineal Descent and Contextual Definition of Status: the Kwaio Evidence." *American Anthropologist* 70:82–84.

Llewellyn, K.N., and Hoebel, E.A. 1941. *The Cheyenne Way*. Norman: University of Oklahoma Press.

Murphy, Robert F. 1964. "Social Change and Acculturation." *Transactions of the New York Academy of Sciences* 26:845–854.

Nimmo, H. Arlo. 1968. "Reflections on Bajau History." *Philippine Studies* 16:32–59.

Republic of the Philippines, Bureau of the Census and Statistics. 1962. *Census of the Philippines 1960: Population and Housing*. Volume 1, "Sulu." Manila: Bureau of the Census and Statistics.

Saleeby, Najeeb M. 1963. *The History of Sulu*. Manila: Carmelo and Bauerman, Inc.

Scheffler, H.W. 1965. "Descent Concepts and Descent Groups: the Maori Case." *Journal of the Polynesian Society* 73:126–133.

Taylor, Carl. 1931. "The Sea Gypsies of Sulu." *Asia* 31:8, 477–483, 534–555.

U.S., Naval Oceanographic Office. 1956. *Sailing Directions for the Philippine Islands*. vol. 3. Washington, D.C.: Government Printing Office.

INDEX

Acculturation, 3–5, 91–92

Boat-dwelling Bajau, 9–43
Bride price:
  Boat-dwelling Bajau, 30–31
  House-dwelling Bajau, 73–74

Cemetery islands:
  Boat-dwelling Bajau, 16
  House-dwelling Bajau, 54
Curing ceremonies:
  Boat-dwelling Bajau, 28–29, 42
  House-dwelling Bajau, 73

Divorce, 93
  Boat-dwelling Bajau, 23–24
  House-dwelling Bajau, 61–63

Family alliance unit, 25–33, 67, 69
Fishing:
  crews, 28, 69–71
  communal, 42–43, 78
  cycles, 15, 41, 54, 74–75
Funerals:
  Boat-dwelling Bajau, 16, 31–32
  House-dwelling Bajau, 74

Generalized kindred:
  Boat-dwelling Bajau, 34
  House-dwelling Bajau, 77

Headmen, 95
  Boat-dwelling Bajau, 34, 35, 36, 37, 40–41, 85
  House-dwelling Bajau, 64, 78, 80, 84–86
House-dwelling Bajau, 47–87
Houseboat moorages:
  Sibutu Islands, 49, 51
  Tawi-Tawi Islands, 12–14, 40–43
Household composition, 92
  Boat-dwelling Bajau, 17–19
  House-dwelling Bajau, 57–59

Imam:
  Boat-dwelling Bajau, 37
  House-dwelling Bajau, 81
Incision ceremony:
  Boat-dwelling Bajau, 30
  House-dwelling Bajau, 63, 74
Innovation, 5
Islam, 16, 53–54, 75, 77, 82–83, 96

Kinship terminology, 93–94
  Boat-dwelling Bajau, 38–39
  House-dwelling Bajau, 65

Localized kindred, 95
  Boat-dwelling Bajau, 34–43, 40
  House-dwelling Bajau, 77–81

Maggomboh ceremony:
  Boat-dwelling Bajau, 34–35
  House-dwelling Bajau, 78–79
Marriage ceremony:
  Boat-dwelling Bajau, 30–31
  House-dwelling Bajau, 73–74
Marriage patterns, 93
  Boat-dwelling Bajau, 21–22
  House-dwelling Bajau, 60–61
Mosque, 50, 82

Neighborhoods, 67–75, 94
Nomadic territory:
  Boat-dwelling Bajau, 16
  House-dwelling Bajau, 54–55
Nuclear family:
  Boat-dwelling Bajau, 17–24
  House-dwelling Bajau, 61, 63, 64, 66

Political organization: *see* Headmen.
Public school, 51, 83–84

Residence patterns, 92
  Boat-dwelling Bajau, 19–21